Martyrs
OF THE
KINGDOM

Martyrs

OF THE KINGDOM

HOYT W. BREWSTER, JR.

BOOKCRAFT
Salt Lake City, Utah

*To all those who have given their lives,
or will yet do so,
for the gospel of Jesus Christ.*

Material quoted from publications of
The Church of Jesus Christ of Latter-day Saints
is used by permission.

Library of Congress Catalog Card Number: 90-81496
ISBN 0-88494-740-8

First Printing, 1990

Printed in the United States of America

It is not necessary, in the providence of God, that we should all be martyrs; it is not necessary that all should suffer death upon the cross, because it was the will of the Father that Jesus should so suffer, neither is it necessary that all the Saints of this last dispensation should perish because our prophet perished, but yet it may be necessary that some should, that a sufficient number of faithful witnesses of God and of his Christ should suffer, and even perish by the hands of their enemies, to prove and show unto the world—the unbelieving and unthinking—that their testimony is true, and that they are ready not only to bear testimony in word, but in deed, to sustain and honor their testimony through their lives; and also in their death. . . . No one can give a stronger assurance of his devotion to the principles he has received and which he teaches to his fellowman, than to patiently endure suffering, for their sake, and, if need be, to continue that suffering and endurance even unto death. (JD 21:26.)

—Lorenzo Snow

Contents

CONTENTS

Acknowledgments

While an author spends many hours in solitary research, pondering, praying, and writing, it is recognized that the end product of any worthwhile endeavor is the result of input, encouragement, and support from many. To all who in any way contributed to this book I offer my heartfelt gratitude:

To Cory Maxwell of Bookcraft Publishers for his encouragement that I bring to fruition my research project on martyrs, which was begun many years ago.

To the *Deseret News,* Deseret Book Company, and Bookcraft Publishers for permission to use some of their copyrighted materials.

To the journal and record keepers of the past, without whose meticulous work this volume would not have been possible.

To the editors and behind-the-scenes people at Bookcraft, whose expertise has added so much to the finished product.

Finally, and most important, to my family for their loving support of me and my projects—to my wife Judy and to my children: Kimberly and Russel Carter, Merrilee, Hillary, and M. Hoyt.

Key to Abbreviations

AA	*Ancient Apostles,* David O. McKay
APP	*Autobiography of Parley P. Pratt*
ASWD	*And Should We Die,* The Church of Jesus Christ of Latter-day Saints
AUS	*The "Americanization" of Utah for Statehood,* Gustive O. Larson
BYUS	*BYU Studies,* Brigham Young University
CC	*Carthage Conspiracy,* Dallin H. Oaks and Marvin S. Hill
CHC	*A Comprehensive History of the Church* (6 vols.), B. H. Roberts
CJ	*Colonia Juárez,* Nelle S. Hatch
CM	*California Mormons,* Annaleone D. Patton
CN	*Church News,* The Church of Jesus Christ of Latter-day Saints
CPGP	*Commentary on the Pearl of Great Price,* George Reynolds and Janne Sjodahl
CR	*Conference Reports,* The Church of Jesus Christ of Latter-day Saints
CTC	*The Church in the Twentieth Century,* Richard O. Cowan

DCE   *Doctrine and Covenants Encyclopedia,* Hoyt W. Brewster, Jr.

DeS   *Desert Saints,* Nels Anderson

DN   *Deseret News,* The Church of Jesus Christ of Latter-day Saints

DNTC   *Doctrinal New Testament Commentary* (3 vols.), Bruce R. McConkie

DS   *Doctrines of Salvation* (3 vols.), Joseph Fielding Smith

DSY   *Devotional Speeches of the Year,* Brigham Young University

ECH   *Essentials in Church History,* Joseph Fielding Smith

En   *Ensign,* The Church of Jesus Christ of Latter-day Saints

ETN   *Ensign to the Nations,* Russell R. Rich

FBM   *Fox's Book of Martyrs,* W. B. Forbush (ed.)

HC   *History of the Church* (7 vols.), The Church of Jesus Christ of Latter-day Saints

HJS   *History of Joseph Smith,* Lucy Mack Smith

HR   *The Heavens Resound,* Milton V. Backman, Jr.

IE   *Improvement Era,* The Church of Jesus Christ of Latter-day Saints

JD   *Journal of Discourses* (26 vols.)

JI   *Juvenile Instructor,* The Church of Jesus Christ of Latter-day Saints

KGR   *The Kingdom of God Restored,* Carter E. Grant

LDP   *Life of David W. Patten,* A. Wilson Lycurgus

LDSAZ   *Latter-day Sentinel,* Arizona Edition

LDSBE   *LDS Biographical Encyclopedia* (4 vols.), Andrew Jenson

LDSBD   *Bible Dictionary,* The Church of Jesus Christ of Latter-day Saints

LDP   *Life of David W. Patten,* A. Wilson Lycurgus

LGL   *Life of a Great Leader,* Bryant S. Hinckley

LJT   *The Life of John Taylor,* B. H. Roberts

MCIM   *The Mormon Colonies in Mexico,* Thomas C. Romney

MD   *Mormon Doctrine* (2nd ed.), Bruce R. McConkie

ME   *The Mormon Experience,* Leonard J. Arrington and Davis Bitton

MFP   *Messages of the First Presidency* (6 vols.), James R. Clark (ed.)

MG   *Mormonism in Germany*, Gilbert W. Scharffs

Mill M   *The Millennial Messiah*, Bruce R. McConkie

MJRY   *Memoirs of John R. Young, Utah Pioneer, 1847*, John R. Young

MM   *The Mortal Messiah* (4 vols.), Bruce R. McConkie

MP   *The Missouri Persecutions*, B. H. Roberts

MS   *Millennial Star*, The Church of Jesus Christ of Latter-day Saints

MsHBY *Manuscript History of Brigham Young, 1801–1844*

NB   *Nauvoo the Beautiful*, Cecil E. McGavin

PBD   *Peloubet's Bible Dictionary*, F. N. Peloubet

PHU   *Popular History of Utah*, Orson F. Whitney

RC   *The Restored Church*, William E. Berrett

RCH   *Readings in LDS Church History from Original Manuscripts* (3 vols.), William E. Berrett and Alma P. Burton

RES   *Religious Educators' Symposium*, The Church of Jesus Christ of Latter-day Saints

RFN   *The Rise and Fall of Nauvoo*, B. H. Roberts

SLS   *The Story of the Latter-day Saints*, James B. Allen and Glen M. Leonard

SLT   *The Salt Lake Tribune*

SOY   *Speeches of the Year*, Brigham Young University

SS   *Southern Star*, The Church of Jesus Christ of Latter-day Saints

ST   *The Signs of the Times*, Joseph Fielding Smith

Talmage *Jesus the Christ*, James E. Talmage

TINL   *There Is No Law*, William W. Hatch

TPJS   *Teachings of the Prophet Joseph Smith*

TS   *Times and Seasons*, The Church of Jesus Christ of Latter-day Saints

WM   *The Women of Mormondom*, Edward W. Tullidge

WTP   *The Way to Perfection*, Joseph Fielding Smith

WV   *Women's Voices*, Kenneth W. Godfrey, et al.

YWJ   *Young Woman's Journal*, The Church of Jesus Christ of Latter-day Saints

Introduction:
The Meaning of Martyrdom

Martyrdom! The very mention of the word conjures up mental pictures of poignant and dramatic moments in man's history. Consider, for example, the Maid of Orleans, who rose from her humble beginnings and youthful inexperience in 1429 to arouse and rally the French people in their struggle for freedom. Though her mortal life ended in fiery flames, Joan of Arc's firm faith in the Savior of mankind was evident to the last as she looked upon the crucifix held aloft at her request and cried the words, "Jesus! Jesus! Jesus!"

Another of the stirring stories of history is that of the American patriot Nathan Hale. At peril to his life, he worked behind enemy lines during the revolutionary war to gain information vital for the freedom of his fledgling country. Betrayed by a renegade relative, Hale was sentenced to death without benefit of trial. Nor were his requests for a clergyman and a Bible honored before being led to the gallows. Though he died without the benefit of an embrace or comforting word from family or friend, his recorded remarks will never be forgotten: "I only regret that I have but one life to lose for my country."

To those who have been personally touched by the untimely death of a loved one whose life has been cut short by an assassin,

1

the word *martyrdom* can release a flood of emotions. Who can sense the motherly pain experienced by Lucy Mack Smith as she looked upon the lifeless corpses of her martyred sons, and who can know the anguish felt by their widows and suddenly fatherless children?

While few have been as deeply touched as was the Smith family in terms of multiple martyrdoms, when any life is lost because of intolerance, disbelief, anger, or hatred, the collective impact upon humanity is immeasurable. Who can measure what the world loses when the life of a man or woman of high principle and great promise is cut short?

Beyond the loss of talent and leadership that might have benefited mankind is the loss of love, compassion, and caring service that could have been rendered. And what of the loss to the martyr of his or her potential posterity? What children might have come through the lineage of one whose life was cut short by an assassin?

Some might argue that putting religious or patriotic zealots and leaders to death is not martyrdom. Perhaps. Yet, dictionaries define a martyr as one who willingly accepts death or the threat of death rather than renounce a firmly held principle or practice.

In this sense, some pretty infamous and vile people might be classified as martyrs, for there have been many wicked men and women whose evil practices have precipitated their deaths. However, in this book the term *martyr* will be used to identify only those individuals whose lives have been taken in causes of righteousness, or whose courses have received divine approbation.

In this respect, consider the following definition of martyrdom:

> In the gospel sense, *martyrdom* is the voluntary acceptance of death at the hands of wicked men rather than to forsake Christ and his holy gospel. It is the supreme earthly sacrifice in which a man certifies to his absolute faith and to the desires for righteousness and for eternal life which are in his heart. . . .
>
> True martyrs of religion receive eternal life. "Whoso layeth down his life in my cause, for my name's sake, shall find it again, even life eternal." (D&C 98:13; Mark 8:35; John 12:25; Rev. 2:10.) But the mere laying down of one's life standing alone is not gospel martyrdom. Both the righteous and the

2

wicked have and do sacrifice their lives for friends or country without gaining thereby any hope or assurance of exaltation. Those on the other hand who have the truth and who could escape death by denying it are the martyrs who shall receive a martyr's reward—eternal life. When they seal their testimony with their blood, they are honored and their murderers are condemned. (D&C 136:39.) (MD, 469-70.)

A martyr's "voluntary acceptance of death" may not always be passive, for one may righteously resist life-threatening situations. For example, Joseph and Hyrum Smith and their companions in Carthage Jail sought to defend themselves against their armed attackers. The ancient prophet Nephi armed his people with swords lest they should be destroyed by those who hated them and their principles (2 Nephi 5:14; Jacob 7:24-25).

Whether a person resists or is passive in the face of impending death, the key question in determining martyrdom is "Could this have been prevented by denying or forsaking righteous principles and beliefs?" If the answer is affirmative, then the death must be classified as martyrdom.

Not all martyrs die directly at the hands of their detractors. Andrew Jenson, who served as the assistant Church historian for many years, identified three classes of martyrs in The Church of Jesus Christ of Latter-day Saints:

1. Saints who have been put to death violently by mobs.
2. Missionaries who died in the field of natural causes or accidents.
3. Pioneers and emigrants, many of whom were cruelly driven from comfortable homes, who crossed the plains and seas in search of refuge with the main body of Saints. (CR, October 1925, p. 54.)

Of this last group, Elder Bruce R. McConkie asked: "Is a saint any less a martyr who is driven from a sick bed into blizzards to freeze and die than he would have been had an assassin's bullet brought merciful death in a brief destroying moment?" (MD, 470.)

Andrew Jenson described the heavy mantle of martyrdom worn by the early pioneers when he wrote, "There is scarcely a mile between Nauvoo, Illinois, and Salt Lake City, Utah, which would not have been marked by graves of the Latter-day Saints who fell as martyrs by the wayside, if a knowledge of their resting places had been preserved" (CR, October 1925, p. 53).

Indeed, one railroad company courteously changed the course of some railroad tracks when it was discovered that the originally charted route would have passed over the clearly marked grave of a pioneer woman. If the graves of all who were laid to rest on the plains had been identified, and the same respect were given to each of them, the pattern of many railroad lines might have been considerably different.

Included in the category of pioneer martyrs, or perhaps added as a fourth category of Church martyrs, might be those who suffered an early and untimely death because of persecution. These are those whose health was broken as a result of tormentors having deprived them of the normal comforts of home and the love and fellowship of friend and family. Samuel H. Smith is a classic example of this.

"On the day a malicious mob murdered his brothers, Joseph and Hyrum, Samuel was relentlessly pursued by a contingent of that mob. Because of the severe fatigue brought on by that chase, a fever was contracted which, according to John Taylor, 'laid the foundation for his death.' " (DCE, 536; see also HC 7:111.)

In the ensuing pages, we will identify and discuss the circumstances surrounding the deaths of martyrs in the kingdom of God from the time of Abel to the present. The purpose of this work is not to evoke sorrow, and certainly not to spark retribution, but rather to honor those who have sacrificed their all in the cause of Christ.

Not all martyrs are known and honored in mortality. In this respect I draw an analogy to the tragic events of 8 October 1871.

On this day the great Chicago fire took the lives of three hundred people. The tragedy received wide news coverage and publicity. To this day it is remembered as one of our nation's more spectacular and tragic events. Yet an even greater tragedy occurred on that same day that went almost unnoticed by the people of that time period and is virtually unknown by those of our day. On 8 October 1871 another raging fire roared through the town of Peshtigo, Wisconsin, claiming more than 1,300 lives. Because the

4

inferno also destroyed the telegraph lines—the major source of communication in those days—the catastrophe was not reported until later. By then, the now famous Chicago fire had taken all the headlines.

In similar fashion, while the names and stories of some great Saints are related in the few pages of this book, many more marvelous martyrs will remain unnamed and unrecorded in print. They are no less important and their eternal reward is just as great as the martyrs whose names are more visible on the mortal marquees of recorded history. These unknown or unnamed martyrs have their names recorded in the Lamb's book of life.

There is yet another group of individuals who deserve our admiration. These are those who were willing to lay their lives on the altar of martyrdom, but who were spared. Included here are people such as Willard Richards, who offered to be hanged in the place of the Prophet Joseph Smith, should the latter have been so condemned, and who survived the brutal attack that claimed the Prophet's life. Consider the many men and women who have suffered severely through the years because of their undeviating desire to remain true to truth and divine principle, who may have been brought to death's door but were not required at that time to pass through.

Among these Saints are Shadrach, Meshach, and Abednego, who refused to relinquish their worship of the true and living God and bow down to a golden image. They were committed to following the commandments of their heavenly King rather than bowing to the decrees of an earthly king. When he cast them into the fiery furnace, their tormentor said, "Who is that God that shall deliver you out of my hands?" In response, the faithful trio replied: "If it be so, our God whom we serve is able to deliver us from the burning fiery furnace, and he will deliver us out of thine hand, O king."

Noting the possibility that their lives might not be preserved, but reaffirming their total commitment to the Lord God, they continued: "But if not, be it known unto thee, O king, that we will not serve thy gods, nor worship the golden image which thou hast set up." (Daniel 3:14–18.)

God intervened in their behalf and their lives were spared to continue their mortal missions. Others were not as fortunate in escaping death by fire. We grieve over the Christians whom the nefarious Nero used as human torches to light his garden. And we are saddened by Alma's account of the men, women, and children who were cast into the fire because of their belief in God (Alma 14). Yet are the three Hebrew men saved from a fiery death any less worthy of the martyr's crown than those whom the fires of martyrdom have consumed?

Perhaps the significance of martyrdom is not found in the act itself but in the character revealed by those who come face to face with such a possibility. One possessed of true faith stands firm amid the fires of affliction and persecution and is refined and strengthened as steel passing through a furnace. On the other hand, those whose character is flawed, who possess faltering or fleeting faith, cannot stand the heat and crumble as clay that has been improperly cured.

The capacity to endure and remain faithful is inherent within each of us as children of God. The choice of cultivating that capacity is up to each of us individually. May we learn from those who have preceded us and follow their example in paying the price required of them.

Part I

ANCIENT
MARTYRS

CHAPTER ONE

Old Testament Times

When the Lord finished the creation of the earth, He pronounced it "good" (Genesis 1:31). For a time there was peace as man and beast shared Eden's serenity. When Adam and Eve partook of the forbidden fruit and were cast out of the garden, the world changed. It would be at least six millenia before the lamb and lion would once again lie down in peace; during these years, mankind would see few periods of peace.

The First Martyr

No one knows how many years passed from the time of the fall of man until the first of God's children suffered death at the hands of one of his brothers. The Old Testament gives limited information about the family of Adam and Eve. The book of Genesis mentions only two sons—Cain and Abel. However, a more complete account is found in the book of Moses. Here we are taught that Adam and Eve conceived and brought forth many sons and daughters prior to the birth of the two children whose tragic story has received so much notoriety (Moses 5:1–3).

Cain was a tiller of the soil; his brother Abel was a keeper of the sheep. It was not their occupations, however, that made these two brothers so different. It was their focus of worship.

Abel worshiped the Lord and "walked in holiness" before Him (Moses 5:26), while his wayward brother Cain loved Lucifer (Moses 5:18). Satan succeeded in getting a foothold among some of the children of Adam and Eve "and they loved Satan more than God" (Moses 5:13). Cain was one who fell into this snare, rejecting the "greater counsel which was had from God" and aligning himself with the master of deceit and evil (Moses 5:18–31).

Abel "brought of the firstlings of his flock" and made an offering to the Lord, which offering the Lord accepted. At Satan's behest, Cain also "brought of the fruit of the ground an offering unto the Lord." When God rejected his hypocritical and evil offering, Cain became angry. Part of this anger was focused on his righteous brother Abel. His bitterness, combined with his coveting the flocks of Abel and his love of wickedness, led Cain down perdition's path of no return. Entering into a murderous pact with the devil, who promised to deliver Abel into his hands, Cain slew his brother, and the blood of the earth's first martyr seeped into her soil (Moses 5:32–33).

The Prophet Joseph Smith exclaimed, "Abel was slain for his righteousness" (TPJS, 260). President Joseph F. Smith saw "Abel, the first martyr" among the "great and mighty ones" assembled among the righteous in the spirit world (D&C 138:38, 40).

The life which Cain took from his brother was restored when Abel participated in the first resurrection that occurred following the resurrection of Jesus Christ. Furthermore, his righteousness has earned him an eternal place in the kingdom of God where he shall receive a fulness of the Father's blessings (D&C 93:19–20).

On the other hand, he who momentarily gloried in his murderous misdeed shall suffer an eternity of sorrow. Speaking of those who seemingly glory in sin, Elder Neal A. Maxwell noted that "the raucousness and shouting of sin, the Cain-like glorying in it, is also the sound of pain trying to erase itself" (1976 DSY, 199).

President Joseph Fielding Smith summed up the tragedy of Cain as follows: "The saddest story in all history is the story of

10

Cain. Born heir to an everlasting inheritance in righteousness, with the promise of a crown of glory that would never fade away, and that too, in the morning of creation when all things were new —and he threw it all away!" (WTP, 97.)

What can be learned from Cain's demise? His descent into the darkness of the devil's domain did not occur suddenly; rather, it was the result of a series of wrong choices which created fatal flaws in his character. He was unwilling to accept counsel and divine reproof. Cain was filled with anger. Being lifted up in pride he sought for position, power, and possessions at the expense of another. He turned his heart from the Father of truth to the father of lies; consequently, Cain will share in the misery of Lucifer and his evil legions throughout eternity.

More Martyrs

We do not know how many martyrs there were between the time of Abel and the great flood. During this period there were some murders that were *not* martyrdoms. For example, Lamech, like Cain before him, entered into a murderous covenant with Satan and slew Irad, who had revealed this secret pact to others (Moses 5:47–50; see also CPGP, 172–73).

At the time of Noah there was great wickedness upon the earth and men thought on evil continually (Genesis 6:5; Moses 8:22). Some murderous men sought to take the life of Noah, but "the power of the Lord was upon him" and his life was spared, for his mortal mission was not yet complete (Moses 8:18). The flood cleansed the earth of the wicked for a time (Genesis 7–8).

Sacrifices in the Days of Abraham

The great patriarch Abraham was forced to flee the land of his fathers because of the threats to his life. On one occasion he was placed upon a sacrificial altar to be slaughtered as an offering to false gods, and, according to the apocryphal book of Jasher, on another occasion he was cast into the fire of the Chaldees (Abra-

11

ham 1:12–17; see also facsimile no. 1; TPJS, 260). Because of the work he was yet to accomplish on this earth, God intervened and saved Abraham's life.

Others were not as fortunate as this ancient prophet. The sacrificial worship of false gods by the people from whom Abraham came took the lives of many men, women, and children (Abraham 1:5–10). Three courageous virgins are specifically mentioned as being sacrificed because "of their virtue; they would not bow down to worship gods of wood or of stone, therefore they were killed" (Abraham 1:11).

There is a lesson to be learned from the martyrdom of the three virgins. They stood for virtue in the face of stiff opposition and dire consequences to themselves.

What does this mean to the Saints of our day? Consider the courageous adults, youth, and even children who refuse to bow down and participate with the world in worshipping the false gods of immorality. Are not immoral behavior, lewd language, immodest dress, sensual movies, suggestive music, rank humor, and all other vile and filthy things examples of false gods of our day?

It is better to be shunned by society and seek for the approval of God than to touch, think, talk of, view, and participate in unclean things. And what of materialism? Is that not another false god of our day? What about lying, cheating, and being dishonest in any way, including falsifying information and reneging on contractual obligations?

Perhaps none in our day will suffer martyrdom for standing firm in the face of a wave of worldly ways. But such stalwarts will be strengthened and come to be worthy of someday entering the celestial kingdom to join with the three virgins of Abraham's day and other martyred Saints who remained true in the face of adversity.

Infant Deaths

Some of the saddest examples of man's inhumanity have been those occasions when the lives of helpless and innocent babies have been taken by the wicked. Lucifer laughs with great pleasure when he destroys a mortal life—something he will never have.

He must find a particularly sickening sense of satisfaction when the taking of a life involves an infant, or, as in abortion, an unborn baby. This deprivation of life strikes at the wellspring of God's plan to people the earth.

One of the earliest occasions when wicked men sought to destroy the plans of God was when Pharaoh, fearing the growth of the people of Israel, ordered the midwives to kill all Israelite male children at birth. God-fearing midwives ignored his evil edict, explaining to the frustrated monarch that the mothers-to-be were so strong that the children were born before the midwives arrived in the birthing room. However, Pharaoh then "charged all his people, saying, Every son that is born ye shall cast into the river." (Exodus 1:7–22.)

Moses escaped this death because of his mother's love and the rescuing hand of Pharaoh's daughter, who took the infant as her own and raised him in the safety of Pharaoh's house (Exodus 2).

Ancient Israel

That the taking of lives was a problem among ancient Israel is evidenced by the laws and regulations that governed the shedding of blood. From the slopes of Sinai, the Lord's voice thundered, "Thou shalt not kill" (Exodus 20:13). The penalties for manslaughter (the unintentional taking of a life) and for murder were spelled out in detail (Numbers 35). There were even ceremonial procedures to be carefully followed when murdered victims of unknown assailants were discovered (Deuteronomy 21:1–9).

We do not know how many of these murder victims would qualify as martyrs, but undoubtedly there were those who forfeited their lives rather than renounce their principles.

While his wicked ways tarnished his own character and crown, King Saul's murderous rage brought a martyr's crown to many. He became insanely jealous of his loyal subject David and sought to slay him (1 Samuel 18–19). When the priest Ahimelech prayed for David and provided him with food and the sword of Goliath, Saul's anger erupted in a flow of martyr's blood. He slew not only Ahimelech but also eighty-four of his fellow priests. His thirst for bloody revenge was not slaked with these deaths, for "Nob, the

13

city of the priests, smote he with the edge of the sword, both men and women, children and sucklings, and oxen, and asses, and sheep." (1 Samuel 22.)

The rage of royalty against prophets and priests of God was also evidenced in the actions of the Phoenician princess Jezebel. She married Ahab, king of Israel, which marriage, "more than any other single event, caused the downfall of the northern kingdom, as Jezebel introduced into Israel the worst forms of Phoenician [idol] worship in place of the worship of Jehovah" (LDSBD, 713; see also 1 Kings 18:4, 13, 19; 19:1–2). Her hatred of the true and living God and His prophets led Jezebel to slay unnamed and unnumbered holy servants of God (1 Kings 18:4, 13; 2 Kings 9:7). It was only through the intervention of the little-known but courageous Obadiah that one hundred other prophets were prevented from suffering a martyr's death at the hands of this wicked woman. She also sought the life of the prophet Elijah, who, having escaped her clutches, claimed he was the lone survivor among all the prophets at that time (1 Kings 18:22).

Zechariah, the prophet-son of Jehoiada the priest, was slain by the idolatrous king Joash. Acting under the direction of the Spirit of God, the prophet called Joash and his people to repentance for worshipping false gods and for their other wicked ways. "And they conspired against him, and stoned him with stones at the commandment of the king in the court of the house of the Lord" (2 Chronicles 24:20–21).

Jeremiah and His Contemporaries

During the days of the prophet Jeremiah there were "many prophets, prophesying unto the people that they must repent, or the great city Jerusalem must be destroyed" (1 Nephi 1:4). One of these prophets was a man named Lehi. His efforts at calling the people to repentance were mocked by the Jews and they "sought his life" (1 Nephi 1:18–20). The Lord protected Lehi and led him and his family to another land, where he became the father of a great civilization whose history is recorded in the Book of Mormon.

14

Jeremiah remained among the Jews and, like other prophets, suffered at the hands of those whom he was trying to help. He was cast into prison (1 Nephi 7:14; Jeremiah 37:15) and lowered by cords into a miry dungeon, where he might have died had not Ebed-melech the Ethiopian intervened in his behalf (Jeremiah 38:6–13).

On one occasion he was arrested and threatened with death for preaching repentance to the people and warning them of their impending destruction. Jeremiah responded to the threats upon his life by saying, "If ye put me to death, ye shall surely bring innocent blood upon yourselves, . . . for of a truth the Lord hath sent me unto you to speak all these words in your ears" (Jeremiah 26:15). Perhaps more out of fear than from faith in his words, the people set Jeremiah free.

Another prophet who preached the same warning message as Jeremiah was not as fortunate. Shortly after Jeremiah's acquittal, the prophet Urijah's life was threatened by Jehoiakim, king of Judah. Urijah fled to Egypt for safety but was pursued and brought back to Jerusalem, where the king "slew him with the sword, and cast his dead body into the graves of the common people." (Jeremiah 26:20–23.)

Martyr-Prophets Not Mentioned in the Bible

There are at least two martyr-prophets who lived in Old Testament times but who are not mentioned in current biblical manuscripts. When the prophet Lehi fled Jerusalem around 600 B.C., he took with him a record known as the brass plates of Laban. Among the things recorded on these plates were the five books of Moses and the words of the prophets from the time of Adam to Jeremiah (1 Nephi 5:10–14). Included among those prophets were Zenos and Zenock.

These two prophets probably lived sometime between the days of Abraham and the ministry of Isaiah (Helaman 8:19–20). The prophet Zenos is mentioned twelve times in the Book of Mormon and the prophet Zenock is mentioned five times. The ancient inhabitants of the Americas whose history is recorded in the Book of Mormon were descendants of these two prophets (3 Nephi 10:16–17).

Both prophets knew and testified of the coming of Christ and bore strong witness of the Son of God (1 Nephi 19:10; Alma 33:12–17). One wonders why their testimonies did not survive the editing process that produced our current Bible. Could it be that the plain and precious truth of their personal witnesses was deliberately deleted (1 Nephi 13:34–40)?

These prophets, like others before and after them, sealed their testimonies with the giving of their lives. Because of his bold testimony Zenos was slain by those who opposed the work he propounded (Helaman 8:19). Similarly, Zenock was stoned to death because the people would not accept his testimony of the Son of God (Alma 33:17). An ancient prophet recorded that many who testifed of the coming of Christ "were slain because they testified of these things" (3 Nephi 10:15).

Probable Martyrs

Another great Old Testament prophet, Isaiah, wrote and testified of the coming of the Messiah in the meridian of time and at the beginning of the Millennium. He prophesied for forty years in Jerusalem (approximately 740–701 B.C.). His writings were the most quoted of the Old Testament prophets by the stalwarts of New Testament times—Jesus, Peter, Paul, and John. Isaiah is also quoted extensively in the Book of Mormon, and when the resurrected Redeemer appeared to the ancient inhabitants of America He declared, "Great are the words of Isaiah" (3 Nephi 23:1).

"Tradition states that [Isaiah] was 'sawn asunder' during the reign of Manasseh; for that reason he is often represented in art holding a saw" (LDSBD, 707).

There were obviously other prophets and righteous people who suffered martyrdom during Old Testament times but who have not been identified. There are a number of New Testament references to these killings (e.g., Matthew 23:29–31; Luke 13:34; Acts 7:52; 1 Thessalonians 2:15). Though unknown to us,

God will undoubtedly grant to each the eternal reward of a martyr.

Divine Intervention

There were instances in Old Testament times when the Lord intervened in behalf of his prophets. The inability of the pharaohs to slay Moses both at birth and later in life is a prime example (Exodus 2; 10:28; 14:1–31).

The story of faithful Daniel whose worship of God caused him to be cast into a den of lions is another great example of divine intervention. When he was discovered alive the morning after his confinement, Daniel declared: "My God hath sent his angel, and hath shut the lions' mouths, that they have not hurt me: forasmuch as before him innocency was found in me" (Daniel 6:22).

Another marvelous manifestation of the Lord's protecting power was with the prophet Elisha. When he saw the hosts of men, chariots, and horses which the king of Syria had sent to capture the man of God, the servant of Elisha fearfully asked his master what they should do. "Fear not," declared the prophet, "for they that be with us are more than they that be with them." Elisha prayed that the lad's eyes might be opened, "and the Lord opened the eyes of the young man; and he saw: and, behold, the mountain was full of horses and chariots of fire round about Elisha." (2 Kings 6:8–17.)

How often does one feel alone when standing for what is right, when in reality the Lord is very near at hand! A Saint will not always be spared suffering, sorrow, and even martyrdom, but in all instances God is mindful of the circumstances of His children and will succor and strengthen the faithful.

CHAPTER TWO

New Testament Times

The Slaughter of the Infants

Among the most notorious names of infamy is that of Herod the Great. Filled with wickedness, this evil ruler put his own wife to death in a fit of jealous rage and later murdered her two sons and the son of another wife. He was also responsible for slaying "nearly all of the great national council, the Sanhedrin. His reign was one of revolting cruelty and unbridled oppression." (Talmage, 98.)

His atrocities reached a terrible peak when, feeling threatened by prophecies of a new king being born among the Jews, Herod insanely ordered the butchering of all the babies of "Bethlehem, and in all the coasts thereof, from two years old and under" (Matthew 2:16).

God warned Joseph and Mary to take their newborn child and flee to Egypt. As a result, *the* Babe of Bethlehem, the One Herod had sought to slaughter, was spared.

While we weep for the loss of the infants brutally torn from the bosoms of their mothers, we find comfort in the doctrine of salvation for little children. Almost two centuries after the slaughter of the infants, He who was saved on that occasion, now acting in His rightful role as the resurrected Redeemer, revealed the following doctrine of comfort: "All children who die before they arrive at the years of accountability are saved in the celestial kingdom of heaven" (D&C 137:10).

Further Effects of Herod's Brutality

At least one other infant escaped Herod's evil edict, a child named John who would have the title "the Baptist" added to his name in his mature years. He was born to parents who were well beyond the normal childbearing years, and—as was the case with the annunciation to Mary of the coming of the Christ child—John's impending birth was announced by the angel Gabriel (Luke 1).

The child's birth was met with great rejoicing by the happy parents as well as their extended family and neighbors. The father, Zacharias, had been told by a heavenly messenger that his son was destined to be a great prophet among the people. He was "to make ready a people prepared for the Lord" (Luke 1:17). Herod's heinous order, decreeing death to all male infants under the age of two, put this mission in jeopardy.

Zacharias hid his infant son from the executioners and refused to disclose the child's whereabouts. As a result, the wicked Herod decreed that the father should forfeit his life.

"According to apocryphal writings, when faced by Herod's threat, Zacharias said: 'I am a martyr of God if thou sheddest my blood; for my spirit the Lord shall receive, because thou sheddest innocent blood in the forecourt of the temple of the Lord' " (DCE, 656).

Over thirty years later, Christ referred to the death of this faithful father as He spoke of the blood shed by martyrs from Abel to Zacharias (Matthew 23:35).

A Belated Martyr's Crown

Although his father's courage had spared him for his ministry of preparing the way before the Lord (John 1:19–28; D&C 84:28), John the Baptist would yet wear a martyr's crown.

19

John spoke out against the "marriage" of Herod Antipas the tetrarch (ruler of a portion of a country) to his half-brother Philip's wife, Herodias. She left her former husband to live with Herod Antipas, and John was unflinching in reproving them for this illegal and illicit relationship. Unwilling to accept this public castigation, and perhaps at his wife's insistence, Herod imprisoned John. (Mark 6:17–18; Luke 3:19–20.)

Herodias would have had John killed immediately, but "Herod feared John, knowing that he was a just man and an holy [man]" and for a time protected the prophet (Mark 6:19–20). In her hatred, Herodias devised a devilish plan to trap Herod into ordering the execution of the prophet whose words had seared her soul.

She had her daughter Salome dance seductively before Herod to the point that he foolishly offered her anything she wanted, even half of his kingdom. The mother and daughter conspired to ask for the head of John the Baptist. Although Herod "was exceeding sorry; yet for his oath's sake, and for their sakes which sat with him, he would not reject her [request]." (Mark 6:21–26.) This is a classic case of an individual taking a wrongful course of action because of social pressure and lustful desires.

The cowardly and foolish ruler sent the executioner to the prison where John was beheaded. His severed head was then placed on a large platter and given to the seductive Salome, who in turn gave it to her wicked mother. (Mark 6:27–28.)

John the Baptist became the first known Christian martyr to die during Christ's earthly ministry. Thus ended the mortal mission of the prophet of whom the Savior said, "Among them that are born of women there hath not risen a greater than John the Baptist" (Matthew 11:11).

An important part of this martyr's ministry would continue following his death. John was one of those Saints who rose from the dead following the resurrection of the Savior (Matthew 27:52). Almost two thousand years later he would once again prepare the way of the Lord. As one of the most significant premillennial events preceding the Second Coming, the resurrected John the Baptist appeared to the Prophet Joseph Smith and Oliver Cowdery in 1829 and bestowed upon them the Aaronic Priesthood (D&C 13; 27:8).

While Herod and Herodias wait in hell for the day of final judgment, John the Baptist has continued to serve on both sides of the veil the Master in whose service he died.

The First Martyr Following Christ

The first known martyr following the crucifixion of Christ was Stephen, one of seven men chosen by the Apostles to assist them in their ministry. He was "a man full of faith and of the Holy Ghost," who was unwavering in the work he was called to perform. A priesthood bearer of great power, he "did great wonders and miracles among the people." (Acts 6:1–8.)

His witness was spoken with such wisdom and spirit that while his detractors rejected his testimony they were unable to refute his words. Although their own spirits might have been in darkness, those who took exception to Stephen's preaching and sat in council against him could not deny the light which filled this man of God, for they "saw his face as it had been the face of an angel" (Acts 6:15).

Angered over his boldness in calling them to repentance, and accusing him of blasphemy because their impure eyes could not see the vision of the Father and Son which Stephen beheld, the people "cast him out of the city, and stoned him." It is of interest to note that one of Stephen's last statements prior to his martyrdom was a reminder that the ancestors of his accusers had persecuted and slain previous prophets. (Acts 7:51–60.)

The magnanimity of this martyr was evidenced in his final words as he "cried with a loud voice, Lord, lay not this sin to their charge." Thus the servant followed the example of the Master, who in His dying hour had similarly said, "Father, forgive them; for they know not what they do" (Luke 23:34).

The persecution did not end with Stephen's death, for Luke tells us that "at that time there was a great persecution against the church which was at Jerusalem; and they were all scattered abroad throughout the regions of Judaea and Samaria" (Acts 8:1). It is reported that the persecution was so severe that martyrdom claimed about two thousand Christians, including

21

Nicanor, who was also one of the seven selected to assist the Apostles (FBM, 2; Acts 6:5).

The First Apostolic Martyr

The first of Christ's inner circle of special witnesses to suffer martyrdom was the Apostle James. He had served as one of the three chief Apostles who held the keys of the kingdom and directed the affairs of the Church (DS 3:152). Together with Peter and John, he experienced the sacred events on the Mount of Transfiguration with the Savior (Matthew 17:1-9). These three were later invited to accompany Jesus into Gethsemane, where a significant part of the Atonement occurred (Matthew 26:36-46).

James was a victim of the venom that spewed from the wicked king Herod Agrippa I in his relentless rage against the early Church (Acts 12:1-2). The mellowing effect of the gospel in James's life was obvious at the moment of his martyrdom. Whereas once he had sought to bring a consuming fire down upon those who had rejected the Master and His message (Luke 9:51-56), he now blessed one who had wronged him. It is alleged that he readily forgave the man whose accusation brought him to the executioner's sword: "As James was being led to the place of execution, this [man] threw himself at the apostle's feet, and humbly begged forgiveness for what he had said against him.

"Putting his arm around the penitent man, James answered, 'Peace, my son, peace be unto thee, and pardon of thy faults.'

"Both were then executed by order of the cruel Herod." (AA, 96.)

Persecution in Pergamos

Pergamos was home to one of "the seven churches of Asia" to which John the Revelator wrote in chapters 2 and 3 of the book of Revelation. In his message, the Revelator, speaking in behalf of the Savior, commends the Saints at Pergamos for remaining faithful in the face of severe persecution, including the martyrdom of one of their members: "I know thy works, and where thou dwellest, even where Satan's seat is: and thou holdest fast my name, and hast not denied my faith, even in those days wherein Antipas was my faithful martyr, who was slain among you, where Satan dwelleth" (Revelation 2:13).

While we do not know anything more about the martyr Antipas than his name, it is sufficient that the Lord knows who this faithful man is. As for the reference to "Satan's seat," Bible commentators give several possibilities. One theory holds that, because a temple was built in Pergamos and dedicated to Rome and her emperor Augustus, the city became the center of imperial worship and thus a throne or *seat* for Satan. Another theory suggests that "Satan's seat" refers to a form of worship practiced there which used the serpent as its emblem. Yet another theory suggests it was Satan's seat because of the severe persecution of the Christians that took place there.

Other Apostolic Martyrs

The manner of death which befell the other Apostles is not recorded in scripture. However, there is much apocryphal evidence to indicate that all but John the Beloved became martyrs (FBM; PBD).

It is reported that Philip was scourged and crucified about A.D. 54. Jude, who is identified by some historians as the Apostle Lebbaeus Thaddaeus or Judas "not Iscariot," was crucified about A.D. 72. Bartholomew suffered a severe beating before he was nailed to the martyr's cross. Andrew is said to have been crucified in Patrae in Achaia on a transverse cross (a cross that is made at right angles to the anterior-posterior axis of the body), which is the origin of the St. Andrew's Cross. The Apostle Simon, who was known as the Canaanite (Matthew 10:4) and Zelotes (Luke 6:15), is reported to have been crucified in Britain in A.D. 74.

Peter, who had pledged to lay down his life for the sake of the Master (John 13:36–38), was probably slain in Rome between A.D. 64 and 69. There is a strong tradition that the Apostle was crucified with the cross in an inverted position. It is alleged that Peter felt himself unworthy to be put to death in the same manner as the Savior and, therefore, requested that he be placed on the cross with his head downward.

In one of his epistles Peter mentions that the Lord had shown him his forthcoming death (1 Peter 1:14). In this respect, it is interesting to note the words of the resurrected Redeemer to His chief Apostle regarding this event: "When thou wast young, thou girdest thyself, and walkedst whither thou wouldest: but when thou shalt be old, thou shalt stretch forth thy hands, and another shall gird thee, and carry thee whither thou wouldest not. This spake he, signifying by what death he should glorify God." (John 21:18–19.)

The Apostle Matthew, to whom we owe great gratitude for recording significant portions of the story surrounding Christ's birth, is said to have suffered martyrdom in the city of Nadabah about A.D. 60. He was apparently slain with a weapon known as a halberd, which is a battle axe mounted on a long handle. Thomas, who because of one incident is sometimes unfairly associated with one who doubts or wavers, was a stalwart for the faith and paid the price by being slain with a spear.

Matthias, who was chosen to replace the fallen Judas (Acts 1:15–26), is said to have suffered martyrdom by being stoned and then beheaded. Another Apostle who was not among the original Twelve to suffer martyrdom was James, the brother of Jesus (Galatians 1:19). It is said that at the age of ninety-four he was beaten with a club and stoned. Another martyr who was referred to as an Apostle was Barnabas (Acts 14:14). He is reported to have been killed around A.D. 73.

Paul is the best known of the Apostles called after the crucifixion of Jesus. His epistles and travels are well chronicled in the New Testament, where he bears a strong and consistent witness of Christ. Paul paid a heavy price for his faithfulness. He was lashed with a whip on at least five occasions, receiving thirty-nine lashes each time. Three times he was beaten with rods and once was stoned and left for dead. He was in constant peril, imprisoned, and suffered great personal deprivation during his ministry (Acts 11:23–28).

24

The Apostle knew of his impending death and wrote what could be a creed for any who face persecution and possible death because of their commitment to the cause of Christ:

But watch thou in all things, endure afflictions, do the work of an evangelist, make full proof of [i.e., fulfill] thy ministry.

For I am now ready to be offered, and the time of my departure is at hand.

I have fought a good fight, I have finished my course, I have kept the faith:

Henceforth there is laid up for me a crown of righteousness, which the Lord, the righteous judge, shall give me at that day: and not to me only, but unto all them also that love his appearing. (2 Timothy 4:5–8.)

Tradition places Paul among the victims of Nero's persecution. It is said the Apostle was condemned to death by the infamous Roman emperor about A.D. 67 or 68. Paul's Roman citizenship spared him from the slow death of crucifixion or the torture of martyrdom by fire. According to historical accounts, he was beheaded.

There were other reported killings among the disciples who followed the Master in his mortal ministry. Mark, to whom we owe gratitude for the New Testament book that bears his name, was allegedly dragged to pieces by a vicious mob in Alexandria. Luke, another of the authors in the New Testament, is supposed to have been hanged by idolatrous priests of Greece. Timothy, the traveling companion of Paul, is said to have been clubbed to death about A.D. 97 by an infuriated pagan mob whom he had reprimanded.

The Slaughter of Christians

The torture and slayings of untold numbers of the followers of Jesus Christ continued around A.D. 67 with appalling cruelty under the nefarious Nero. He took wicked delight in diabolical deaths. In addition to making a sport of having Christians torn apart by wild beasts, the emperor had some of them sewn in ani-

25

mal skins and then given as playthings to vicious dogs who tore at them until death mercifully released their spirits from their mutilated bodies. Other martyrs were dressed in waxen clothing and set on fire to illuminate the emperor's gardens. Many suffered the traditional crucifixion, and others were tortured to death by having the bones in their bodies broken and crushed.

The Roman emperor Domitian rekindled the intense fires of persecution around A.D. 81. The followers of the Prince of Peace were blamed for any misfortune that befell the empire, including famine and earthquakes. Domitian had a law passed that required Christians who were brought before the tribunal to renounce their religion or be punished. A test oath was proposed that required the death of Christians if they refused to take the oath or if they confessed to being followers of Christ.

Thousands more were put to death under continuing persecutions in the years that followed. Every conceivable cruel and inhumane method was employed to torture and annihilate the Christians, including beheading, burning, branding, burying alive, beating, crushing, crucifying, scalding, stoning, starving, skinning or fileting, being placed on a rack and stretched or torn apart, being forced to run a gauntlet between hunters, and being given as food or fun to wild beasts. One noble martyr, facing his death before the lions, said: "I am the wheat of Christ: I am going to be ground with the teeth of wild beasts, that I may be found pure bread" (FBM, 8).

It is said that the lives of early Christians consisted of "persecution above ground and prayer below ground" (FBM, 11). Beneath the city of Rome were hundreds of miles of catacombs that provided places of prayerful worship for these early Saints. In many instances these underground temples of worship also proved to be the tombs for their dead. When brought to trial, the only so-called "crime" these Christians were accused of committing was meeting together in prayer and covenanting to avoid all forms of wickedness.

In mimicry of the Savior's death, many were crucified with crowns of thorns on their heads and had their ordeal ended by having spears thrust through their sides. It is reported that because one highly honored Roman commander refused to join in this slaughter that he and his family were ordered to be killed along with the Christians.

Before their deaths, some martyrs were scourged until their sinews and veins lay bare; others were forced to walk repeatedly over sharp objects that shredded their bare feet. One venerable old man refused to refute Christ as a condition for clemency with these stirring words: "Eighty and six years have I served him, and he never once wronged me; how then shall I blaspheme my King, Who hath saved me?" (FBM, 9.)

Additional waves of violent persecution and death continued to pour over the Christians during the following centuries. Such persecution was not confined to the Roman empire, but spread to other areas where the prince of darkness sought to destroy the children of light.

The martyrdoms of those who held the keys of authority for Christ's kingdom on earth, perhaps combined with the killing of so many faithful Saints who might have risen to positions of leadership and done much good in the world, were factors that allowed the church that Christ had established to slip into apostasy. For centuries mankind would be without the full light of the gospel. As foreseen by the Revelator, the Church had been driven into the wilderness for a time (Revelation 12:6, 14).

Those wicked or misguided mortals who aided the work of the adversary have their dark acts recorded in the annals of infamy while the names of their faithful victims shine with luster in the Lamb's book of life.

The martyred Saints will rise to a glorious resurrection and eternal reward, while their evil antagonists will suffer the demands of justice. Gone will be the corruptible crowns worn in wickedness and the earthly scepters of power exercised unrighteously. In their place will be chains of darkness (D&C 38:5). While the wicked wear the shackles of sin that bind them to Satan, the righteous whom they persecuted will have their brows adorned with eternal crowns of glory and receive everlasting thrones and kingdoms (D&C 29:13; 121:29).

CHAPTER THREE

Christ As a Martyr: The Ransom for Mankind

While the death of any martyr must not be minimized, there should be universal recognition that the Martyr who mattered most was our Lord and Savior, Jesus Christ.

The death of the first martyr, Abel, had been one of particular sorrow, separation, and despair, but the shedding of the blood of "Jesus the mediator [spoke] better things than that of Abel," for His holy blood represented hope, resurrection, and renewal of life (Hebrews 12:24).

The Savior taught of His sacrifice when He said, "The Son of man came not to be ministered unto, but to minister, and to give his life a ransom for many" (Matthew 20:28). Peter added this reminding witness of the Redeemer: "Ye know that ye were not redeemed with corruptible things, as silver and gold, . . . but with the precious blood of Christ, as of a lamb without blemish" (1 Peter 1:18–19).

From the moment of His birth in Bethlehem, His path pointed toward two gardens and a hill. His mortal mission would culminate with the excruciating suffering in Gethsemane's garden and the crucifixion on the cross of Calvary's hill. Yet, three days later the sorrowing Saints would find joy in a quiet garden outside the walls of Jerusalem as they entered the empty tomb and learned that Christ had indeed risen from the dead.

The Path of Persecution and Rejection

Hundreds of years before the birth of the Babe of Bethlehem, an inspired prophet foresaw the travails to be suffered by the Son of God:

> He is despised and rejected of men; a man of sorrows, and acquainted with grief: and we hid as it were our faces from him; he was despised, and we esteemed him not.
> Surely he hath borne our griefs, and carried our sorrows: yet we did esteem him stricken, smitten of God, and afflicted.
> But he was wounded for our transgressions, he was bruised for our iniquities: the chastisement of our peace was upon him; and with his stripes we are healed. (Isaiah 53:3-5; see verses 3-12.)

Little is known of the first thirty years of this Man among men. That He may not have seemed much out of the ordinary to His neighbors is evidenced by their reactions when He later returned to "his own country." They were astonished at the wisdom of His words when He taught in the local synagogue. "Is not this the carpenter?" they asked. "And they were offended at him." Because of their unbelief, Jesus "could there do no mighty work. . . . And he marvelled because of their unbelief." (Mark 6:1-6.)

When Jesus quoted the messianic words of Isaiah to the people of Nazareth, applying the prophecy directly to His ministry, the townspeople "were filled with wrath, and rose up, and thrust him out of the city, and led him unto the brow of the hill whereon their city was built, that they might cast him down headlong." Because His mission on earth was not yet complete, these would-be murderers were prevented from carrying out their evil designs on this occasion. (Luke 4:16-30.)

Later the Jews in Jerusalem were offended because Jesus healed a man on the Sabbath who had suffered from a crippling malady for thirty-eight years. Rather than recognize the hand of God in this miracle, and misunderstanding the greater law which was fulfilled in such a healing, the people narrowly focused on the letter of the law, which restricted Sabbath day activities. "And therefore did the Jews persecute Jesus, and sought to slay him, because he had done these things on the sabbath day. But Jesus answered them, My Father worketh hitherto, and I work. Therefore the Jews sought the more to kill him, because he not only had broken the sabbath, but said also that God was his Father, making himself equal with God." (John 5:16–18; see verses 1–23.)

Still on another Sabbath Jesus healed a man with a withered hand. On this occasion the disbelievers deliberately watched the Compassionate One to see if He would heal the afflicted man "on the sabbath day; that they might accuse him."

Knowing their evil intent, Jesus confronted them with this soul-searching question: "Is it lawful to do good on the sabbath days, or to do evil? to save life, or to kill?" Unable or unwilling to respond to the question that must have seared their scarred consciences, His detractors "held their peace." Yet, "the Pharisees went forth, and straightway took counsel with the Herodians against him, how they might destroy him." (Mark 3:1–6; see also Matthew 12:10–14; Luke 6:6–11.)

Because of their lack of sensitivity to the witness of the Spirit, the Pharisees rejected the testimony of Jesus and accused Him of bearing false witness. They might have sought to slay Him but "no man laid hands on him; for his hour was not yet come." (John 8:12–20.) He who had been honored in premortal councils in preference to the devil was now accused of being possessed of a devil (John 10:19–20). He was charged by others with healing by the power of the chief of the devils (Luke 11:14–15).

Following in the ways of the master tempter, the devil himself, there were those who sought to tempt Jesus to unrighteously display His powers over life and the elements of nature (Luke 11:16; compare Matthew 4:1–11). This He steadfastly refused to do, reminding these sign seekers that "an evil and adulterous generation seeketh after a sign" (Matthew 12:38–40).

His authority to minister and teach was challenged (Matthew 21:23). And the evidences of His authority were rejected: "But though he had done so many miracles before them, yet they believed not on him" (John 12:37). Pharisaical predators constantly but unsuccessfully pounced on His words, seeking to snare Him in their ill-concealed traps of twisted meanings: "And as he said these things unto them, the scribes and the Pharisees began to be angry and to urge vehemently, endeavoring to provoke him to speak of many things; laying wait for him, and seeking to catch something out of his mouth, that they might accuse him" (JST, Luke 11:54-55; see also Luke 20:20; Matthew 22:15; Mark 12:13).

It is ironic that He who proclaimed and practiced principles of peace—returning good for evil, turning the other cheek, loving one's enemy—should Himself become the object of such intense persecution. Plotting against Him continued throughout His short mortal ministry. Herod the king had unsuccessfully tried to kill the newborn Son of Mary. Years later the king's son Herod the tetrarch sought to do what his father had failed to do. In response to this threat, Jesus proclaimed that His death was not to be at the hands of the pagan Herod in Perea but rather at the hands of His own countrymen in Jerusalem. (Luke 13:31-35.)

There are other recorded instances of threats of violence against the Messiah, but each failed, for it was not yet the time for Him to give up His life (Luke 20:19; John 10:30-39). But that day would come, as prophesied by Christ: "Then assembled together the chief priests, and the scribes, and the elders of the people, unto the palace of the high priest, who was called Caiaphas. And consulted that they might take Jesus by subtilty, and kill him." (Matthew 26:3-4.)

Betrayed by a Trusted Associate

For three years Jesus had traveled the dusty paths of Palestine teaching, blessing, healing, and giving counsel and comfort. His every effort was to raise mankind to a higher level of living in this world and to the highest levels of the hereafter.

A dedicated group of disciples followed Him during His ministry, and a few, namely the Twelve Apostles, had a particularly close association with the One who had called them to be fishers of men. This inner group of men shared intimate moments and received counsel and authority which others did not experience. Theirs was perhaps one of the most noble and loving associations ever experienced by a brotherhood of men.

Yet, among this group of elite and special witnesses, there arose a traitor to Christ and to the cause. What led to the downfall of Judas Iscariot is not fully known, but one comment by an apos-

31

tolic colleague leads us to conclude that Judas's slide to sin was not sudden happenchance. John the Beloved recorded that on the occasion when Mary anointed Jesus' feet with costly ointment, Judas objected. Judas suggested that the ointment might have been sold and the money given to the poor. On the surface this may have seemed a charitable gesture, but Judas had a dark motive: "This he said, not that he cared for the poor; but because he was a thief, and had the bag [the money purse for the Twelve], and bare what was put therein." (John 12:1–6.) Evidently Judas had been pilfering from the purse entrusted to his care.

For about one-third of the cost of the precious ointment, Judas would soon sell his soul: "Then one of the twelve, called Judas Iscariot, went unto the chief priests, and said unto them, what will ye give me, and I will deliver him unto you? And they covenanted with him for thirty pieces of silver. And from that time he sought opportunity to betray him." (Matthew 26:14–16.)

Yet even as Judas stood on the brink of damnation, a loving Savior offered him a chance to repent. During the eating of the paschal meal, Jesus said, "One of you which eateth with me shall betray me" (Mark 14:18). Could it be that this public announcement was an opportunity for the perpetrator to turn from perdition's path, to confess and forsake the error of his ways? Whatever the reason for the announcement, Judas unfortunately did not rise to the occasion.

Even as he left the supper to do his deed of darkness, Judas's identity as the traitor appeared to be safeguarded by the Man he sought to betray. Jesus merely said, "That thou doest, do quickly. Now no man at the table knew for what intent he spake unto him." (John 13:27–28.) Was this yet another opportunity for Judas to save face as well as his soul?

The next time Jesus and the other Apostles saw Judas the traitor was when he arrived at their secluded meeting spot leading a mob armed with swords and staves to arrest the Sinless One.

Gethsemane's Ordeal

Following the institution of the sacrament among His chosen disciples and giving them further instructions and counsel, Jesus prayed mightily in behalf of His Apostles in particular and the

Saints in general (John 17). This personal plea to His Holy Father has been called the Lord's High-Priestly Prayer. In it the Savior acknowledges the Father's preeminent position and gives an accounting of His stewardship: "I have glorified thee on the earth: I have finished the work which thou gavest me to do" (John 17:4).

It is not certain whether all of this took place in the upper room where the Last Supper was eaten or if portions of the discourse and prayer occurred outside. The place is of little consequence. The message is critical. When He had concluded His pleadings with His Father, Jesus and the eleven Apostles sang a hymn and went out to the Mount of Olives. An inspired account of this occasion tells us that "the disciples began to be sore amazed and to be very heavy, and to complain in their hearts, wondering if this be the Messiah."

It is ironic that as Jesus was on the very threshold of fulfilling His messianic role to save mankind from death and hell (2 Nephi 9), there should be any question in the hearts of His disciples about His being the Messiah, the Anointed One, the Christ. Knowing their hearts and feeling the beginnings of the awful weight that was to be laid upon Him, Jesus rebuked them and then said: "My soul is exceedingly sorrowful, even unto death." (JST, Mark 14:36–38.)

Arriving at Gethsemane, He left the eight others and invited His three chief Apostles to accompany Him a little farther, where He asked them also to remain and to watch and pray that they enter not into temptation. Knowing that the full power of the tempter was soon to be unleashed upon Him (see Talmage, 613), could the Savior have been forewarning His Apostles that the power of the evil one would soon be unleashed in the garden?

Jesus then retired to the sacred seclusion of Gethsemane to enter the first painful hours of His eternal atonement. Notwithstanding the paintings which depict Him leaning against a rock or tree serenely supplicating His Father, for at least part of the time Jesus was on His face, praying in great pain, prostrate on the ground. "Abba" (a word expressive of combined affection and honor, signifying Father), He cried, "all things are possible unto thee; take away this cup from me." Then was added the supreme example of humble submission to any assignment given from God, "Nevertheless not what I will, but what thou wilt." (Mark 14:36.)

Three times Jesus would interrupt His prayerful pleadings to go back to the place where He had left the three Apostles; each time He would find them asleep. The first two times Jesus awakened them, reminding them to "watch and pray, that ye enter not into temptation," and then gently adding, "the spirit indeed is willing, but the flesh is weak" (Matthew 26:41). Upon finding them asleep a third time, the Sufferer let them sleep while His approaching captors arrived.

We learn much about personal prayer in times of trial from the Savior's struggle in Gethsemane. Each time He left the rebuked Apostles He resumed His pleadings with the Father. When His own discomfort was not relieved, He did not succumb to self-pity, wane in His resolve to complete His mission successfully, or complain against or reject God; rather, *"being in an agony he prayed more earnestly"* (Luke 22:44; italics added). What a marvelous example of supernal faith in His Father! In the Father's wisdom, and to the eternal blessing of all mankind, this suffering but obedient Son would not be spared this experience.

As He prayed, "there appeared an angel unto him from heaven, strengthening him" (Luke 22:43). One author has suggested that this angel might well have been mighty Michael, known on earth as Adam, who successfully led the battle against Lucifer in the pre-earth battle for men's souls (MM 4:125). Would it not be appropriate for the precipitator of the Fall in Eden's garden to be here on the occasion of the Atonement in Gethsemane's garden?

A few brief words are all that the New Testament tells us about the extent of the Savior's suffering: "His sweat was as it were great drops of blood falling down to the ground" (Luke 22:44). Fortunately there is other inspired commentary of this sacred occasion when the Lord "offere[d] himself a sacrifice for sin" (2 Nephi 2:7). An ancient prophet recorded, "He suffereth the pains of all men, yea, the pains of every living creature, both men, women, and children, who belong to the family of Adam" (2 Nephi 9:21). Another wrote that Jesus would "take upon him the pains *and* the sicknesses of his people" (Alma 7:11; italics added).

Almost two millennia after He suffered for our sins, sorrows, sicknesses, pains, and all the torment that Satan could inflict upon

34

Him on that occasion, the resurrected Redeemer personally spoke of His anguished experience:

> For behold, I, God [Jesus Christ or Jehovah], have suffered these things for all, that they might not suffer if they would repent;
> But if they would not repent they must suffer even as I;
> Which suffering caused myself, even God, the greatest of all, to tremble because of pain, and to bleed at every pore, and to suffer both body and spirit—and would that I might not drink the bitter cup, and shrink—
> Nevertheless, glory be to the Father, and I partook and finished my preparations unto the children of men. (D&C 19:16–19.)

We are told by Elder Bruce R. McConkie, one of His modern-day Apostles, that this suffering beyond compare continued "for some three or four hours" (En, May 1985, p. 9).

Another of the Savior's special witnesses, Elder James E. Talmage, noted: "It was not physical pain, nor mental anguish alone, that caused Him to suffer such torture as to produce an extrusion of blood from every pore; but a spiritual agony of soul such as only God was capable of experiencing. . . . In that hour of anguish Christ met and overcame all the horrors that Satan, 'the prince of this world' could inflict." (Talmage, 613.)

"Thus ends such accounts as we have of Jesus' suffering in Gethsemane. It is now over and he has won the victory; the atonement, in large measure, has been worked out, and he is now ready for the shame and humiliation and pain of the cross. Then will come the resurrection and the crown." (MM 4:126.)

Arising from the ground, His clothing and flesh stained with bloody sweat and the soil upon which He had suffered, Jesus awoke the disciples and said, "Rise, let us be going: behold, he is at hand that doth betray me" (Matthew 26:46).

Betrayed, Forsaken, and Denied

Following the ordeal in Gethsemane, Christ was now ready for the next part of His sacred atonement. As He and His chosen associates conversed quietly in the garden, Judas approached at the head of a large crowd which included Roman soldiers and Jewish religious leaders. On this occasion Judas misused the token of love and friendship—a kiss—to treacherously betray Jesus. The Savior's gentle but rebuking words to this feigned friend were, "Judas, betrayest thou the Son of man with a kiss?" (Luke 22:48.)

Although there was a moment following His arrest when the Savior's friends and associates stood by Him, we are told that "all the disciples forsook him, and fled" (Matthew 26:56). Peter followed the throng from a distance (Matthew 26:58) and one young man, whom we assume to be Mark, followed closely enough that he was recognized and seized, but he was able to break free of their grasp and flee (Mark 14:51–52).

The sole Christian captive on this night was Christ Himself.

There followed a series of trials and examinations that made a mockery of justice. He who was without sin was first brought before the deposed high priest Annas (John 18:14), a man described as evil, wicked, and adulterous. One chronicler wrote that Annas "ranks with Judas among the abominable of the earth" (MM 4:143).

Then Jesus was taken before the incumbent—or shall we say incompetent—high priest, Caiaphas, and members of the ruling religious body, the Sanhedrin. Here He whose lips never uttered a lie listened to the accusing testimony of many false witnesses. Throughout this specious spectacle "Jesus held his peace," saying nothing until the high priest demanded: "I adjure thee by the living God, that thou tell us whether thou be the Christ, the Son of God?"

Jesus' simple and straightforward answer was, "Thou hast said," which was the equivalent of saying, "I am what thou hast said." (Matthew 26:63–64.)

This was a declaration to these pretenders to authority that they indeed stood in the presence of the Son of God, *the* true High Priest, He who really had authority from God, the promised Messiah, the King of kings. Lacking the spiritual sensitivity to recognize the Royal One who stood before them, His audience rejected Him. Instead of falling on bended knee in acknowledgment of Christ's regal role, they "began to spit on him, and to cover his face, and to buffet him, and to say unto him, Prophesy: and the servants did strike him with the palms of their hands" (Mark 14:65).

While Jesus was suffering this humiliation within the house of Caiaphas, His chief Apostle Peter waited outside. This seemingly stalwart disciple who had taken up the sword to defend Jesus at the time of His arrest was soon to feel the stinging reality of Christ's earlier utterance to him that Peter would soon thrice deny the Master.

As Peter tried to stand inconspicuously with others warming themselves by a fire in the courtyard, he was approached by a young woman who recognized him as one of the followers of Jesus. Peter denied knowing Him or being one of His disciples and withdrew himself from the group. As he did so, the sound of a cock crowing could be heard. A little later another woman identified Peter as one of Christ's companions and again he denied it. About an hour later Peter was once more confronted regarding his association with Jesus, and he vehemently denied it.

"And the second time the cock crew. And Peter called to mind the word that Jesus had said unto him, Before the cock crow twice, thou shalt deny me thrice. And when he thought thereon, he wept." (Mark 14:72.)

From this bitter experience was born a new resolve on Peter's part. Never again would he falter in the face of death or adversity. Hereafter he would remain true to his testimony in boldly declaring Jesus to be the Christ, the Son of the living God.

Mocked and Rejected by Jew and Gentile

The ordeal of Jesus' mock trials and hearings continued during the night and into the early morning hours of the next day. He was formally condemned by the Sanhedrin in the morning in a deceitful attempt to ratify their illegal actions of the night before. Christ's forced appearance before this religious tribunal during the previous night, as well as the proceedings of that occasion, were contrary to Jewish law.

Following His ironical conviction of blasphemy, the Jews led the rejected Jehovah to be judged and condemned by the Gentiles. Jesus was first taken to Pilate, the appointed Roman governor or procurator of Judea, Samaria, and Idumea. Because a Jewish tribunal did not have the authority to legally pronounce the death penalty, the Sanhedrin sought the permission of Pilate (Talmage, 627; John 18:31).

This puppet ruler of Rome asked what charges were brought against the Prisoner before him. Christ's accusers knew that charges of blasphemy would not be acceptable to the pagan Pilate, so they tried to evade the question by replying, "If he were not a malefactor, we would not have delivered him up unto thee." Pilate, probably seeing through their thinly veiled hatred of an innocent Man, told them to take Jesus and judge Him according to their law. Their response was that it was not lawful for them to put a man to death. The Apostle John then records that this was said in order that Christ might suffer the prophesied death. (John 18:28–32.)

Regarding this statement, Elder James E. Talmage noted the following:

> John the apostle intimates in this last remark a determination on the part of the Jews to have Jesus put to death not only by Roman sanction but by Roman executioners; for, as we readily may see, had Pilate approved the death sentence and handed the Prisoner over to the Jews for its infliction, Jesus would have been stoned, in accordance with the Hebrew penalty for blasphemy; whereas the Lord had plainly foretold that His death would be by crucifixion, which was a Roman method of execution, but one never practised by the Jews. Furthermore, if Jesus had been put to death by the Jewish rulers, even with governmental sanction, an insurrection among the people might have resulted, for there were many who believed on Him. The crafty hierarchs were determined to bring about His death under Roman condemnation. (Talmage, 632–33.)

Several days before the feast of the Passover, Jesus had foretold the forthcoming manner of His death: "The Son of man is [to be] betrayed to be crucified" (Matthew 26:2). Centuries before this, Enoch had been shown in vision "the Son of Man lifted up on the cross" (Moses 7:55). Other Old Testament prophets

38

had prophesied of the wounds that would be in the hands and feet of the Savior as a result of His manner of death (Psalm 22:16; Zechariah 13:6).

The resurrected Redeemer later affirmed that His whole mission in mortality pointed toward the cross: "And my Father sent me that I might be lifted up upon the cross; and after that I had been lifted up upon the cross, that I might draw all men unto me, that as I have been lifted up by men even so should men be lifted up by the Father, to stand before me, to be judged of their works, whether they be good or whether they be evil" (3 Nephi 27:14).

It is of interest to note that having announced their intentions to have Jesus put to death, His accusers changed the charge from blasphemy to high treason. "To the vociferous accusations of the chief priests and elders, the calm and dignified Christ deigned no reply. To them He had spoken for the last time—until the appointed season of another trial, in which He shall be the Judge, and they the prisoners at the bar." (Talmage, 633.)

Pilate commenced to question the Prisoner, asking Him if He were the King of the Jews. Jesus responded by saying His kingdom was not of this world, but affirmed that He indeed was a King. Following their brief dialogue, Pilate announced to the Jews that he found no fault in Jesus. Clamoring for His conviction, the Jews cried that Jesus had stirred up trouble from Galilee to Judea. Upon learning that Jesus was a Galilean, Pilate sought to rid himself of the responsibility of judgment by sending the Captive to Herod Antipas, who was the ruler of that province and who happened to be in Jerusalem at the time.

Herod's efforts to question Jesus were met with stately silence; after mocking Him, this unholy ruler returned the Prisoner to Pilate. "Herod is the only character in history to whom Jesus is known to have applied a personal epithet of contempt ["that fox"]. . . . As far as we know, Herod is further distinguished as the only being who saw Christ face to face and spoke to Him, yet never heard His voice." (Talmage, 636.)

After Jesus was returned to Pilate, the procurator called the chief priests and rulers together and proclaimed that neither he nor Herod had found Jesus to be guilty of the things of which He was accused. Catering in a cowardly fashion to the hatred of Jesus' accusers, Pilate offered to have the innocent Prisoner scourged and then released. This did not placate those who were so filled with hate, for they would not be satisfied with even a bloody beating but only with death.

Once more Pilate sought a ploy to release the innocent Man who stood bound before him. It was the custom for the governor to pardon and release a condemned prisoner at the Passover. Pilate offered the people a choice of Barabbas, a man convicted of sedition and murder, or Jesus, whom both he and Herod had found innocent of such crimes.

Even Pilate's wife knew of Jesus' innocence and sent a message to her husband as he sat on the judgment seat: "Have thou nothing to do with that just man: for I have suffered many things this day in a dream because of him. But the chief priests and elders persuaded the multitude that they should ask Barabbas, and destroy Jesus." (Matthew 27:19–20.)

Succumbing to the will of the maddened mob, Pilate released Barabbas and turned Jesus over to the soldiers to be scourged prior to His crucifixion. This beating of His bare back was done with a whip whose thongs were loaded with metal and jagged pieces of bone so that the lashes would actually tear at the flesh as they were administered. Many victims of this punishment did not survive it.

The soldiers were not satisfied with the blood which poured from their Victim's torn back. To add to their fiendish pleasure they mockingly dressed Him in a purple robe, forced a crown of thorns upon His brow, and placed a reed in His hands. "Hail, King of the Jews," they cried as they struck Him and covered Him with their filthy spittle.

With Jesus in this sorrowful condition, Pilate paraded Him before the people in one more attempt to sway them, to evoke some semblance of sympathy and mercy that would lead to His release. "Behold, the man," Pilate said as he pointed to the pitiful Prisoner. "Pilate seems to have counted on the pitiful sight of the scourged and bleeding Christ to soften the hearts of the maddened Jews. But the effect failed. Think of the awful fact—a heathen, a pagan, who knew not God, pleading with the priests and people of Israel for the life of their Lord and King!" (Talmage, 639.)

With minds darkened with evil rage, the people cried out for the death of Him who was the Light and Life of the world (3 Nephi 11:11; see also Isaiah 9:2; John 8:12; 12:46). The rejecting cry of apostate Israel was, "We have no king but Caesar" (John 19:15). And so it was that Pilate washed his hands of the whole affair and turned Christ over to the people to be crucified.

It is of interest to note that in spite of his efforts to free Jesus, Pilate did not escape culpability in decreeing the death of Jesus. He simply succumbed to the pressure put upon him by those who threatened to report him to Rome. Such a complaint might have exposed his past misdeeds of corruption and cruelty and brought about his removal from office, perhaps even punishment and imprisonment.

In fear of such action, he added one more wrong to his history. Elder Neal A. Maxwell noted that "Pilate's hands were never dirtier than just after he had washed them" (En, November 1974, p. 13).

The Crucifixion

A man condemned to be crucified was forced to walk to the place of crucifixion while carrying the cross upon which his body was to be nailed. Having suffered indescribable agony in Gethsemane the previous night, and then being subjected to the physical and emotional torment inflicted on Him by His detractors, Jesus was in a very weakened condition. He was evidently unable to carry the load on His back or to move as fast as the impatient crowd wanted. The soldiers therefore forced a man called Simon of Cyrene to carry the cross the remaining distance to Calvary.

Those who participated in the procession included those who had condemned and rejected their Messiah, the morbid, the curious, and some genuine mourners, particularly women. The only recorded words that Jesus spoke during this tragic trek were those he addressed to these weeping women: "Daughters of

Jerusalem, weep not for me, but weep for yourselves, and for your children" (Luke 23:28). He went on to tell them that their own future trials would be so terrible that women would wish to be barren so that they would not see their children suffer.

The path of the procession continued through a portal of the walls of Jerusalem to a small hill just beyond. This site was known as Golgotha, which was the Hebrew word for "the skull" (John 19:17). The Latin translation of this word, which Luke uses, is Calvary (Luke 23:33).

Two merciful acts commonly provided those condemned to be crucified were not granted the Savior. One consisted of giving the sufferer a blow under the arm pit that hastened his death; the second consisted of giving the condemned some wine that had been mixed with a powerful opiate that would help alleviate the suffering. For whatever reason the first was not offered, and the second was rejected by the Savior Himself (Matthew 27:34; MM 4:210). Suffering as He was, He chose to be in full control of His senses to the end.

About 9:00 A.M. on Friday morning, the cross was laid on the ground and the sign which Pilate had ordered written in three languages—Greek, Latin, and Hebrew—was hung thereon, proclaiming: "JESUS OF NAZARETH THE KING OF THE JEWS." This was probably Pilate's way of embarrassing the priests and elders who insisted on His death. (John 19:19–22.)

Being stripped of His clothing, Jesus was stretched upon the cross and huge iron nails were driven through sensitive nerves in His hands, wrists, and feet, crushing tendons as they tore through the flesh (David B. Haight, En, Nov. 1989, p. 60). Centuries before this moment, a prophet had messianically testified that Christ should be fastened "as a nail in a sure place" (Isaiah 22:23). There was a wooden projection near the center of the cross to partially support the weight of the tortured body and keep it from tearing through the nails and off the cross.

When the cross was tortuously raised to its upright position and set firmly in the ground, the Crucified must have suffered as the jarring movement sent shocks of pain through His body. These pains intensified as the minutes and hours dragged on for the Sufferer.

42

In contrast to His pureness and innocence, Christ was crucified between two malefactors, both guilty of crimes and perhaps deserving of death. An ancient prophet had seen and testified of this trio of victims, only One of whom qualified as a martyr (Isaiah 53:12). It is likely that the Savior's cross was elevated slightly above the other two as it occupied the center position.

Contrary to many paintings depicting the Crucifixion, the Victim was close enough to the ground that vicious hands could reach out and strike a blow of hatred. On the other hand, the gentle touch of compassion from a courageous loved one might also be felt stroking broken and bleeding feet. There were undoubtedly among this crowd a compassionate few who looked with pity upon their King and offered prayers and words of comfort in His behalf.

However, the spiritual sickness of many continued to manifest itself as they looked upon the suffering Son of God and in ridicule said, "Save thyself, and come down from the cross." They reminded the crowd that Christ had saved others, and asked why He could not save Himself and come down from the cross so that they might believe. (Mark 15:29–32.)

He hung there in regal silence, practicing what He had preached, not returning railing for railing but literally turning the other cheek to be smitten again (Matthew 5:39; see also 1 Peter 3:9).

He was devoid of any earthly possessions, for His garments had been gambled away by the soldiers who were His executioners.

During the six hours of His torture on the cross, seven utterances came from His holy lips. Each reveals something about the Man whom millions worship.

His *first utterance* was directed to Him whose sired Son He was: "Father, forgive them; for they know not what they do" (Luke 23:34). Elder Bruce R. McConkie noted that this plea applied only to the Roman solders who were simply carrying out their duty and not to the wicked priests and rulers who had abused and condemned Him (MM 4:211). Forgiveness for the specific act of crucifixion was sought, not total absolution from all sins, for that would have to occur in the same way as it does for all men—through proper repentance and baptism.

43

This gives understanding to the *second statement* uttered by the suffering Savior. One of the malefactors, perhaps in a desperate bid to save his own life, if that were possible, or perhaps suffering the effects of his own sins and hate, began to rail away at the Savior in mimicry of the mob: "If thou be the Christ, save thyself and us." He was in turn rebuked by his fellow transgressor, who reminded him that they deserved what they were getting but that Jesus was an innocent Man.

Turning his head toward the Savior he implored, "Jesus, Lord, remember me when thou comest into thy kingdom." Jesus responded by saying, "Today shalt thou be with me in paradise." (Luke 23:39–43.) This was not a promise of instant salvation, as some have supposed. The Prophet Joseph Smith said the statement meant, "This day thou shalt be with me in the world of spirits: then I will teach you all about it and answer your inquiries" (TPJS, 309).

Christ's *third utterance* was a compassionate request regarding His mother. She who had brought Him into the world, had nurtured and protected Him, now stood helpless at the foot of the cross as she watched the life ebb slowly from her suffering Son. Standing close by her was the beloved disciple, John the Apostle. Perhaps painfully nodding towards John, Jesus said to His mother, "Woman, behold thy son!" Then He charged His disciple "Behold thy mother!" Thus, He placed one loved one in the care of another. (John 19:26–27.)

At midday, the forces of nature reacted to the scene of their suffering Creator, and darkness covered the land for three hours. "The darkness was brought about by miraculous operation of natural laws directed by divine power. It was a fitting sign of the earth's deep mourning over the impending death of her Creator." (Talmage, 660.)

About three hours later, Christ's pained voice was heard in the midst of the darkness uttering His *fourth statement*, as recorded in Mark 15:34, "Eloi, Eloi, lama sabachthani?" ("My God, my God, why hast thou forsaken me?") Concerning this expression of anguish, Elder Talmage wrote:

What mind of man can fathom the significance of that awful cry? It seems, that in addition to the fearful suffering incident

44

to crucifixion, the agony of Gethsemane had recurred, intensified beyond human power to endure. In that bitterest hour the dying Christ was alone, alone in most terrible reality. That the supreme sacrifice of the Son might be consummated in all its fulness, the Father seems to have withdrawn the support of His immediate Presence, leaving to the Savior of men the glory of complete victory over the forces of sin and death. (Talmage, 661.)

The *fifth phrase* spoken from the cross was one of physical need: "I thirst." These words, the first relating to His own personal needs, were only spoken after He knew "that all things were now accomplished, that the scripture might be fulfilled." (John 19:28.) Responding to His plea, one who stood by took a piece of sponge which probably served as a cork for a vessel of vinegar-like brew which the Roman soldiers normally drank and, placing it on a reed or stalk, lifted it to the parched lips of the Sufferer. Jesus sipped from the sponge and fulfilled the messianic prophecy: "They gave me also gall for my meat; and in my thirst they gave me vinegar to drink" (Psalm 69:21).

Even as this one took compassion on Jesus, there were yet those heartless onlookers who would have denied the Sufferer His request, tauntingly suggesting such a denial might bring Elias to the rescue.

The *last two utterances* from the cross emphasized the finality of the Savior's earthly mission. "It is finished," He exclaimed (John 19:30). And then, once more addressing Him whose will He came to do, He simply said, "Father, into thy hands I commend my spirit" (Luke 23:46). Even at the moment of death, Christ quoted messianic scripture (Psalm 31:5).

Knowing that He had done all that His Father had sent Him to do, Christ chose the moment of His death. Just hours earlier, the regal Prisoner had told Pilate that the procurator's power was conditional and that Jesus allowed Himself to be held as their captive and to be condemned (John 19:11). Many months before this fateful day Jesus had proclaimed: "No man taketh [my life] from me, but I lay it down of myself. I have power to lay it down, and I have power to take it again." (John 10:18.)

While we mourn this Martyr's suffering and death, we recognize that it was purposeful. Three days later His spirit and body

45

would reunite as the first fruits of the resurrection. Because of His death and resurrection all martyrs and all mankind have hope of a resurrection. With the Apostle Paul we triumphantly cry, "O death, where is thy sting? O grave, where is thy victory?" (1 Corinthians 15:55.)

Before His body was taken from the cross and hastily placed in a borrowed tomb, His lifeless body would suffer one more humiliation, and yet bear one more witness. A spear was thrust in His side to attest to His death, "and forthwith came there out blood and water." Sensing the significance of this occurrence, the Apostle John then bore his solemn witness of what he had just seen. (John 19:34–35.)

> Why does John, as though he were recording some great miracle, tell us that both blood and water flowed from Christ's pierced side, and then add his solemn certification that he spoke the truth in so stating? It appears that the Beloved Disciple was showing how one of the great doctrines of revealed religion, that of being born again, rests upon and is efficacious because of the atonement. As the inspired record recites, men are "born into the world by water, and blood, and the spirit" thereby becoming mortal souls. To gain salvation they must thereafter "be born again into the kingdom of heaven, of water, and of the Spirit, and be cleansed by blood," meaning the blood of Christ. (Moses 6:59.) Thus when men see birth into this world, they are reminded of what is required for birth into the kingdom of heaven. (Bruce R. McConkie, DNTC, 1:834.)

As life and death go on around us, we are daily reminded of why Jesus Christ was indeed the Martyr who mattered most!

We exclaim, as did the soldier at the foot of the cross, "Truly, this man [is] the Son of God" (Mark 15:39).

CHAPTER FOUR

Book of Mormon Times

Those Who Might Have Been Martyrs

Throughout the history of mankind there might have been more martyrs had not the Lord intervened on occasion to protect those whose mission in life was not yet complete. Father Lehi, the progenitor of the people of the Book of Mormon, is one of those whose life was spared. He was a contemporary of the prophet Jeremiah and lived in Jerusalem around 600 B.C.

Hundreds of years before the holy event, Lehi was shown in vision the coming of the Son of God; he was also shown the more immediate destruction of Jerusalem and the scattering of her people. He prophesied of these events and called the people to repentance, but they rejected his plea: "They were angry with him; yea, even as with the prophets of old, whom they had cast out, and stoned, and slain; and they also sought his life" (1 Nephi 1:20).

The Lord protected His prophet and commanded him to take his family and flee Jerusalem. Lehi, his wife, Sariah, and their family were joined in their journey by Zoram, the servant of the wicked Laban, and the family of Ishmael. This little band of refugees was led on a journey that ultimately took them to a new land, where they established a civilization that essentially became two nations—the Lamanites and the Nephites.

The Nephites were originally led by the stalwart prophet Nephi, whose life had been sought on several occasions by those who opposed the work he had been called to do (1 Nephi 7:16; 17:48; 2 Nephi 5:2–5). Each time he was threatened, the Lord delivered Nephi from the hands of his enemies, and he was able to continue his ministry.

Knowing the hatred of those who opposed him and his work, Nephi armed his people with swords so they could defend themselves. The early chapters of the Book of Mormon do not reveal how often these swords had to be used, or how many martyrs might have died in defense of their faith and freedom. That there were such casualties can be assumed by the fact that Nephi tells us that he gives a more complete account of such conflicts in his "other" record, a translation of which we do not currently have (1 Nephi 9:4).

Abinadi's Ordeal

The first recorded death of a martyr in the Book of Mormon as it now exists is that of a bold prophet named Abinadi. He spoke out strongly against the wicked monarch Noah, who with his people reveled in riotous living. The wicked king sought the life of the faithful prophet but was unsuccessful in getting his hands on him for over two years.

Abinadi was finally imprisoned and brought before those who sought to accuse him of wrongdoing, "but he answered them boldly, and withstood all their questions . . . and did confound them in all their words" (Mosiah 12:19). Tiring of Abinadi's words of rebuke, they sought to take him and put him to death, but the prophet was protected until he had finished delivering his message.

"Touch me not," he declared, "for God shall smite you if ye lay your hands upon me, for I have not delivered the message which the Lord sent me to deliver; neither have I told you that which ye requested that I should tell; therefore, God will not suffer that I shall be destroyed at this time" (Mosiah 13:3).

48

The power of the prophet was such that the people dared not touch him. Abinadi spoke with great power and authority, and as he continued his message a physical transformation took place, for "his face shone with exceeding luster, even as Moses' did while in the mount of Sinai, while speaking with the Lord" (Mosiah 13:5).

For some time the prophet reproved the recalcitrant people, reminding them of the commandments of the Lord and urging their repentance. He spoke messianically and bore strong witness of the mission and message of the coming Son of God, declaring "only in and through Christ ye can be saved" (Mosiah 16:13).

Having delivered his message, Abinadi was given a choice of recanting his words or being put to death. His courageous response was, "I will suffer even until death, and I will not recall my words, and they shall stand as a testimony against you. And if ye slay me ye will shed innocent blood, and this shall also stand as a testimony against you at the last day." (Mosiah 17:10.)

At this point, the power of Abinadi's words struck terror into the heart of the wicked king. He "was about to release him for he feared his word; for he feared that the judgments of God would come upon him." But succumbing to the persuasions of the wicked priests whose company he kept, and allowing himself to be swallowed in the quicksand of anger, King Noah decreed Abinadi's death. (Mosiah 17:11–12.)

The prophet was first frightfully beaten by his venomous captors and then consigned to the fiery flames, where he suffered a martyr's death. Even in the grasp of that very painful death, Abinadi continued to preach and prophesy until he cried, "O God, receive my soul. And now, when Abinadi had said these words, he fell, having suffered death by fire; yea, having been put to death because he would not deny the commandments of God, having sealed the truth of his words by his death." (Mosiah 17:19–20.)

To our knowledge, there was only one heart softened by the prophet's words—that of a young priest named Alma. He would later prove to be one of the great prophets of the Book of Mormon. During his ministry he would be responsible for turning thousands to the truth and testimony of Jesus Christ. Thus we see the significance of Abinadi's being spared for even a short time.

The Fate of Faithful Gideon

Following the death of Abinadi, another faithful man arose among the subjects of King Noah, a man by the name of Gideon. He opposed the king and sought his life. However, as Gideon was about to slay the evil monarch, King Noah saw a Lamanite army approaching and begged Gideon to spare his life so he in turn could save his people. "And now the king was not so much concerned about his people as he was about his own life; nevertheless, Gideon did spare his life" (Mosiah 19:8).

Noah's cowardice and wicked ways were ultimately brought to an end when some of his subjects put him to death by fire, as prophesied earlier by Abinadi. Gideon became a respected leader among the people formerly ruled by the wicked King Noah and now governed by Noah's righteous son Limhi. Gideon was the new king's captain of their small military force and devised a plan whereby Limhi's people were able to escape their Lamanite tormentors (Mosiah 22).

He later became a teacher in the Church and was an example of Alma's description of what a true teacher should be: "Trust no one to be your teacher nor your minister, except he be a man of God, walking in his ways and keeping his commandments" (Mosiah 23:14).

Some years later, when he was a much older man, Gideon defended the Church against an anti-Christ named Nehor, using the word of God as his weapon of truth. "Now, because Gideon withstood him with the words of God [Nehor] was wroth with Gideon, and drew his sword and began to smite him. Now Gideon being stricken with many years, therefore he was not able to withstand his blows, therefore he was slain by the sword." (Alma 1:9.)

Thus ended the life of a noble man who had been a true patriot and preacher to his people. He went on to a martyr's reward while he who slew him, who sought to establish his false doctrine by force, was judged for his crimes, executed, and sent to the realms of the damned.

Deaths by Fire

About 82 B.C., "Satan had gotten great hold upon the hearts of the people of the city of Ammonihah" (Alma 8:9). The Lord sent Alma to preach repentance to the inhabitants of that wicked city, but they "withstood all his words, and reviled him, and spit upon him, and caused that he should be cast out of their city" (Alma 8:13).

As he sorrowed over the wickedness of the people, an angel appeared to Alma and directed him to return to Ammonihah and warn the people one more time. In spite of the way he had been mistreated and rejected by the people, Alma did not balk at or seek to be excused from his assignment. Rather, we are told that "he returned speedily to the land of Ammonihah" (Alma 8:18). What a great lesson in obedience!

Upon his return Alma met a man named Amulek, who was receptive to the prophet and his message. After a period of spiritual tutoring, Amulek was called by revelation to accompany Alma in testifying to the people and preaching the word of God. "And they had power given unto them, insomuch that they could not be confined in dungeons; neither was it possible that any man could slay them; nevertheless they did not exercise their power until they were bound in bands and cast into prison. Now this was done that the Lord might show forth his power in them." (Alma 8:31.)

In spite of the power of their words, there were many who hardened their hearts and would not believe or repent. For His own divine purposes, the Lord did not intervene when the two prophets were bound and forced to watch as many martyrs were sacrificed:

> And they brought their wives and children together, and whosoever believed or had been taught to believe in the word of God they caused that they should be cast into the fire; and they also brought forth their records which contained the holy scriptures, and cast them into the fire also, that they might be burned and destroyed by fire.
>
> And it came to pass that they took Alma and Amulek, and carried them forth to the place of martyrdom, that they

might witness the destruction of those who were consumed by fire.

And when Amulek saw the pains of the women and children who were consuming in the fire, he also was pained; and he said unto Alma: How can we witness this awful scene? Therefore let us stretch forth our hands, and exercise the power of God which is in us, and save them from the flames.

But Alma said unto him: The Spirit constraineth me that I must not stretch forth mine hand; for behold the Lord receiveth them up unto himself, in glory; and he doth suffer that they may do this thing, or that the people may do this thing unto them, according to the hardness of their hearts, that the judgments which he shall exercise upon them in his wrath may be just; and the blood of the innocent shall stand as a witness against them, yea, and cry mightily against them at the last day. (Alma 14:8–11.)

Thus, on this frightful occasion, an unnumbered group of believers passed through the portals of death and became martyrs to the cause of Christ. We can imagine that even as some of them still suffered in great pain while the flames seared their skin and sapped the life from their bodies, others at that moment were being greeted in a joyous reunion on the other side of the veil. While one minute these martyrs were crying out in mortal anguish, the next moment cries of joy and praise were likely being heard as they entered the world of righteous spirits.

Alma and Amulek, sorrowing at this painful sight, stood ready to offer their own lives on this occasion but were not called upon to do so.

Converts Who Could Not Be Dissuaded from Their Faith

There were hundreds of thousands, even millions, of war casualties in the Book of Mormon. Many of these deaths could not be considered martyrdoms but rather should be seen as the natural consequences of hatred and wickedness. However, there were those victims of warfare whose faithfulness and loyalty to God surely should mark them as martyrs.

Among these faithful martyrs were the converted Lamanites known as the people of Ammon, or the Anti-Nephi-Lehies. These people were known for their zeal in keeping God's commandments and remaining true to their covenants. So strong was their conviction that they buried their weapons of war and vowed never again to stain their swords with the blood of their fellowmen, even if under attack. "If our brethren destroy us," they said, "behold, we shall go to our God and shall be saved" (Alma 24:16).

"And this they did, it being in their view a testimony to God, and also to men, that they never would use weapons again for the shedding of man's blood; and this they did, vouching and covenanting with God, that rather than shed the blood of their brethren they would give up their own lives" (Alma 24:18).

Their faith was soon put to the severest test, for their former countrymen came against them in an angry attack. Seeing the oncoming army, the people of Ammon prostrated themselves on the ground before the advancing army and began to call upon God. While they were in this attitude of prayerful pleading, the Lamanites began to slay them. "And thus without meeting any resistance, they did slay a thousand and five of them; and we know that they are blessed, for they have gone to dwell with their God" (Alma 24:22).

Why did God not stop this army as He had done when Pharaoh's forces sought to destroy the children of Israel on the borders of the Red Sea (Exodus 14)? Perhaps in His divine wisdom, God saw beyond the outer man and into the hearts of many of the misguided Lamanite soldiers. When these hardened warriors saw that their victims offered no resistance and "praised God even in the very act of perishing under the sword," many of them threw down their weapons and joined in worshiping with the people of Ammon.

"And it came to pass that the people of God were joined that day by more than the number who had been slain; and those who had been slain were righteous people, therefore we have no reason

53

to doubt but what they were saved. And there was not a wicked man slain among them; but there were more than a thousand brought to the knowledge of the truth; thus we see that the Lord worketh in many ways to the salvation of his people." (Alma 24:26–27.)

Although the hearts of many Lamanites were softened, not one of the group of apostate Nephites known as Amalekites turned from his wicked ways (Alma 24:29–30). In their hatred of goodness, they continued to "stir up the people in anger against their brethren, the people of Anti-Nephi-Lehi," and once again caused the deaths of many of these peaceful people (Alma 27:2–3).

More Deaths by Fire

Among the most bitter enemies of the righteous are those who have once known the truth and tasted of the goodness of God but who have fallen away and are now pursuing the path marked out by the enemy of righteousness, even the devil himself. It is written that "after a people have been once enlightened by the Spirit of God, and have had great knowledge of things pertaining to righteousness, and then have fallen away into sin and transgression, they become more hardened, and thus their state becomes worse than though they had never known these things" (Alma 24:30).

Such was the case with the wicked people known as the Amulonites. They perverted the ways of the Lord, taking satisfaction in sin. These disciples of Satan sought to slay those who had turned their lives to the way of truth and "caused that many of the Lamanites [who were converts to the Lord's ways] should perish by fire because of their belief" (Alma 25:5).

Shedding the Blood of Prophets and Saints

The specific details of many martyrdoms are not given in the Book of Mormon, although the victims are mentioned. For example, during the days of darkness that followed the crucifixion of

Christ, the Lord spoke to the surviving inhabitants of ancient America. Among the survivors were some who had either been directly involved in or consented to the slaying and stoning of the prophets (3 Nephi 8:25).

Jesus Christ recounted for them the great destruction which had come upon many cities of the wicked. The inhabitants of these cities had been destroyed because of their abominations and wickedness, including their many murders of the Savior's servants. The Lord declared that He had destroyed these ungodly murderers so "that the blood of the prophets and the saints should not come up unto me any more against them." (3 Nephi 9:5, 7–9.)

He further proclaimed: "And behold, the city of Laman, and the city of Josh, and the city of Gad, and the city of Kishkumen, have I caused to be burned with fire, and the inhabitants thereof, because of their wickedness in casting out the prophets, and stoning those whom I did send to declare unto them concerning their wickedness and their abominations. And because they did cast them all out, that there were none righteous among them, I did send down fire and destroy them, that their wickedness and abominations might be hid from before my face, that the blood of the prophets and the saints whom I sent among them might not cry unto me from the ground against them." (3 Nephi 9:10–11.)

Among those martyrs referred to by the Lord were probably some who lost their lives just prior to the events surrounding the Crucifixion. The record reveals that "there were many of those who testified of the things pertaining to Christ who testified boldly, who were taken and put to death secretly by the judges, that the knowledge of their death came not unto the governor of the land until after their death" (3 Nephi 6:23). The stability of the government was shaken by evil members of secret combinations "who murdered the prophets" (3 Nephi 7:6).

At least one martyr was raised from the dead. Timothy was stoned to death by the unbelievers but was restored to life through the priesthood power and faith of his brother, Nephi (3 Nephi 7:19). One of the reasons for this miracle became apparent when the resurrected Redeemer later chose Timothy as one of His twelve disciples among the Nephites (3 Nephi 19:4).

Martyrs among the Jaredites

About a millennium and one-half before the family of father Lehi came to the Americas, another civilization began on this same soil. The Lord had led a small colony of people to these lands from among those whose language was confused at the Tower of Babel. These people were known as the Jaredites.

For hundreds of years they lived in this new land and were the beneficiaries of words of wisdom from great prophets and leaders. They were also troubled by the words and actions of the wicked among them. Among the worst of their wicked ways was the establishment of oath-bound secret combinations, whose founder was the devil and whose purpose was the destruction of nations and all that is good (Ether 8). The secrets of this satanic society would also surface among the Nephites many years later, causing the deaths of many (Helaman 1:9; 3 Nephi 7:1).

A Jaredite ruler by the name of Heth embraced this secret society and the sin and evil for which it stood. He led his people to do likewise. When the prophets came among them crying repentance, "the people believed not the words of the prophets, but they cast them out; and some of them they cast into pits and left them to perish" (Ether 9:29).

Some years later, in the days of a ruler named Com, prophets came among the people and once again called them to repentance. When the people rejected the prophets and "sought to destroy them," they fled to Com for protection (Ether 11:2). Here they were safe until Com died and the new ruler's brother rebelled against the government and was successful in putting to death all the prophets who had prophesied of the people's destruction (Ether 11:4–5).

It is likely that other prophets and righteous people lost their lives as martyrs before the Jaredite civilization was destroyed, for the people did not repent and instead rejected the prophets who came to them (Ether 11:22). They cast out the last prophet, Ether, who "hid himself in the cavity of a rock by day, and by night he went forth viewing the things which should come upon the people" (Ether 13:13). He wrote of the destruction of the Jaredite civilization and hid the records which would later be translated by the Nephite prophet Moroni.

The Last Nephite Martyrs

Because of wickedness, the Nephite civilization was also destroyed. The prophet-historian Mormon tells us that "there never had been so great wickedness among all the children of Lehi, nor even among all the house of Israel" than existed at the time his nation was destroyed (Mormon 4:12). Yet even amidst such depravity there were those who withstood the flood of filth and evil. Chief among these were Mormon and Moroni and undoubtedly their wives and others of their family.

Mormon wrote to his faithful son, Moroni, and described the horrible atrocities that the people were committing, indicating that they were "without principle, and past feeling; and their wickedness doth exceed that of the Lamanites" (Moroni 9:20). Then, in grateful tribute for the son who remained true to his principles in spite of the wickedness that surrounded him, Mormon said: "But behold, my son, I recommend thee unto God" (Moroni 9:22). Would that all sons and daughters would merit such a recommendation!

Mormon was slain defending his people, and Moroni was one of the last survivors to escape capture and death. In solitude, he continued his inspired work with the sacred records containing the history of his people and, more important, another witness of Jesus Christ. He kept himself hidden during this time of writing and compiling, for the Lamanites sought to kill him and would have destroyed the sacred records entrusted to his care.

The strength of his conviction during these lonely and dangerous times is evidenced in these words: "For behold, their wars are exceedingly fierce among themselves; and because of their hatred they put to death every Nephite that will not deny the Christ. And I, Moroni, will not deny the Christ; wherefore, I wander whithersoever I can for the safety of mine own life." (Moroni 1:2–3.)

Moroni lived long enough to complete his record and hide it safely within a hill named Cumorah. We do not know whether he died a natural death or as a martyr to the cause of Christ. We only know that some fourteen hundred years later, he appeared as a resurrected being to entrust the record he had safeguarded to a modern-day prophet—Joseph Smith. This sacred record, considered as scripture to millions, is another witness of Him whom

Moroni and his father Mormon served, even Jesus Christ. It was published to the world in 1830 as the Book of Mormon.

In order to focus greater attention on its messianic message, in 1982 the subtitle "Another Testament of Jesus Christ" was added to the Book of Mormon (En, November 1982, p. 53).

There would soon be a sequel to the Book of Mormon's history of martyrs, for the prophet, seer, and revelator called upon to translate this ancient record would also seal his work and testimony with his blood.

Part II

LATTER-DAY MARTYRS

CHAPTER FIVE

Persecution of a Prophet Named Joseph

Prophecies of Apostasy and Restoration

Following the martyrdoms of Christ's Apostles in the Old World and the deaths of His chosen disciples on the American continent, priesthood authority and the saving ordinances of the gospel were not available on earth. Without the flow of revelation and prophets to guide them, the early Christians fell into erroneous practices and false beliefs. Doctrines were changed and mankind went through a long period of spiritual darkness. Many good people lived during this time, some of whom even gave their lives in defense of their belief in Christ, but they lacked the fulness of His gospel.

The prophets and Apostles had prophesied of such a condition (Amos 8:11; Acts 20:29; 2 Thessalonians 2:3; 2 Timothy 3:1–7). Yet, there had also been promises of a restoration of the saving principles and ordinances of the gospel of Jesus Christ (Daniel 2:44; Matthew 17:11; Acts 3:21; Ephesians 1:10).

A Prophet Named Joseph

The ancient seer Joseph, who was sold as a slave into Egypt and who later rose as a great leader among the Egyptians and as a prophet among Israel, foresaw the day of restoration and the prophet who would be raised up to direct this important labor (2 Nephi 3). This latter-day leader would be a seer like the ancient prophets Joseph and Moses. He would have power to bring forth the word of God and to confound false doctrines. And his name was to be *Joseph*.

Centuries after Joseph of old uttered this prophecy, on a spring morning in the year 1820, a fourteen-year-old boy named Joseph Smith entered a secluded grove of trees to ask God where he might find the true Church of Jesus Christ. He was confused by the many churches and multiple creeds which, while professing to represent Jesus Christ, were all different from one another. How could such confusion be of God?

Kneeling in humble prayer, the youth began to offer up the desires of his heart. No sooner had he begun than the powers of darkness sought to destroy him and to prevent the promised restoration of the gospel of Jesus Christ.

Joseph said that the power of this enemy from the unseen world was such that his tongue was bound and he could not speak. As the thick darkness gathered around him, the boy thought he was doomed to destruction. At this awful crossroads of despair, the youth exerted all his powers to call upon God in mighty prayer. The power of God prevailed—a pillar of light pierced the grove and the darkness was dispelled. Although the master of darkness who retreated on this occasion would continue his forays against the true faith, never again would the light of the gospel be totally extinguished.

Two glorious Personages appeared to the youth. Joseph records, "One of them spake unto me, *calling me by name* and said, pointing to the other—This is My Beloved Son, Hear Him!" (Joseph Smith—History 1:17; italics added.) (Eight years later, One of these holy Beings would once again call this young prophet by name saying, "Behold, *thou art Joseph*, and thou wast chosen to do the work of the Lord" [D&C 3:9; italics added].) At the time of this first vision, Joseph was told by the Personage who addressed him not to join any of the existing churches or sects because none had a fulness of the gospel or the power to act in God's name. Little is recorded of this sacred theophany, but there is no doubt that young Joseph knew he "was called of God" to a special work (Joseph Smith—History 1:28).

To the Church and to the world, the Lord Jesus Christ would declare: "Wherefore, I the Lord, knowing the calamity which should come upon the inhabitants of the earth, called upon my servant Joseph Smith, Jun., and spake unto him from heaven, and gave him commandments" (D&C 1:17).

The Lord would be the Tutor of this unlearned prophet, revealing through him His divine will. Over the next twenty-four years this work would unfold—a magnificent tapestry whose divine design would slowly unfold under the direction of the master Weaver.

Persecution of a Boy-Prophet

Through the modern-day prophet Joseph Smith, the Lord effected the restoration of the fulness of His gospel, with all its saving ordinances, covenants, and principles. Yet, as was the case with former-day prophets and Apostles, this modern-day prophet would also pay a heavy price for his commitment to the cause of Christ.

From an early age, the adversary was aware of Joseph's potential. In fact, Satan knew long before Joseph Smith was born that he was destined to be one of the Lord's great prophets. Lucifer had led the forces of evil in rebellion against God in the pre-earth life, and Joseph Smith was among the "noble and great ones" who stood and fought valiantly on the side of truth on that momentous occasion (Revelation 12:7–9; D&C 76:25–26; Abraham 3:22–23). As a result of his faithfulness, Joseph was foreordained to come to the earth to fulfill a special calling (HC 6:364).

Satan's efforts to destroy Joseph Smith and the divine work he was destined to perform did not commence with his attack on the young prophet in the Sacred Grove. Joseph said, "It seems as though the adversary was aware, at a very early period of my life, that I was destined to prove a disturber and an annoyer of his kingdom; else why should the powers of darkness combine against me? Why the opposition and persecution that arose against me, almost in my infancy?" (Joseph Smith—History 1:20.)

We know very little about the specifics of the early persecution of which the Prophet speaks, but several examples might illustrate what he endured. There is one recorded instance of someone deliberately shooting at the young boy in the darkness as he walked to his home one evening. Evidence found the next morning indicated that the would-be assailant had been lying in wait. The bullet intended for Joseph inadvertently struck a cow.

As a youngster who had recently undergone painful surgery on his leg, leaving him limping and lame for a time, the boy had been maliciously mistreated by a teamster hired to help the family. The man had compelled Joseph "to travel miles at a time on foot, notwithstanding he was still lame" (HJS, 62).

Both of the above instances occurred prior to Joseph's experience with Deity in the Sacred Grove. Persecution would greatly intensify after the spring of 1820. Joseph soon discovered that telling others about his marvelous manifestation brought intense prejudice against him. He reported that a minister treated his story not only lightly but also "with great contempt."

"I soon found," he said, "that my telling the story had excited a great deal of prejudice against me among professors of religion, and was the cause of great persecution, which continued to increase; and though I was an obscure boy, only between fourteen and fifteen years of age, and my circumstances in life such as to make a boy of no consequence in the world, yet men of high standing would take notice sufficient to excite the public mind against me, and create a bitter persecution; and this was common among all the sects—all united to persecute me." (Joseph Smith—History 1:21–22.)

Opposition to the Book of Mormon

One of the missions Joseph Smith was to accomplish during his life, as prophesied by Joseph of old, was to "bring forth [God's] word" as received and recorded by the posterity of this ancient seer (2 Nephi 3:11–12). This "word" would be a new book of scripture, a companion volume to the Bible. But the bringing forth of the word of God in addition to the Bible would not be well received by many. "A Bible! A Bible!" they would cry. "We have got a Bible, and there cannot be any more Bible." (2 Nephi 29:3.)

Enemies of this inspired new book of scripture would mistakenly or disparagingly often refer to it as the "Golden Bible." This description had reference to the fact that the metal plates upon which this record was recorded "had the appearance of gold" (HC 4:537).

This new record was not another Bible, but a separate witness or another testament of Jesus Christ, known today as the Book of Mormon. The title page of this book states that one of its purposes is "to the convincing of the Jew and Gentile that JESUS is the CHRIST, the ETERNAL GOD, manifesting himself unto all nations."

The bringing forth of this witness of Christ occupied a great deal of Joseph Smith's thoughts, time, and energy from 1823 through 1830. During the first four of these years, the young prophet was being tutored by divine instruction while he was also learning patience.

Joseph learned how desperately the powers of darkness would strive to destroy the plates and the work to which he was called. Moroni, the heavenly messenger who was sent to reveal the plates to the young prophet, warned him that "Satan would try to tempt [him] to get the plates for the purpose of getting rich" (Joseph Smith—History 1:46).

During Joseph's first visit to the place where Moroni had hidden the plates, the youth attempted to remove them from their hiding place. However, three times his efforts to touch or remove the plates were repelled by a jolting shock of some unseen power. "Why cannot I obtain the book?" he cried out. "Because you have not kept the commandments of the Lord," came the reply from the heavenly messenger who now stood by his side.

Moroni reminded Joseph that the sole purpose for getting the plates should be to build the kingdom of God, and the young man's mind had already entertained thoughts that were not consistent with this divine injunction. There followed a vision wherein the budding prophet was shown the prince of darkness and an innumerable group of his evil followers. These wicked ones would fiercely oppose the coming forth of this additional testament of Jesus Christ.

When the Prophet was finally allowed to take possession of the plates in 1827, the hosts of hell were there to oppose him. Brigham Young said, "Do you not think that those spirits knew when Joseph Smith got the plates? Yes, just as well as you know that I am talking to you now. They were there at the time, and millions and millions of them opposed Joseph in getting the plates; and not only they opposed him, but also men in the flesh." (JD 5:55.)

Joseph was attacked by unknown assailants three times on his way home with the plates. In defending himself from the third man the young prophet dislocated his thumb. He prayerfully and carefully safeguarded the plates, for news of their existence traveled like wildfire, and numerous attempts were made to steal them. The Prophet later reported that "as soon as the news of this discovery was made known, false reports, misrepresentation and slander flew, as on the wings of the wind, in every direction; the house was frequently beset by mobs and evil designing persons. Several times I was shot at, and very narrowly escaped, and every device was made use of to get the plates away from me." (HC 4:538; see also Joseph Smith—History 1:60.)

An Attempt to Destroy Priesthood Power

During the time the Book of Mormon was being translated, Joseph Smith received visitations from important heavenly messengers. Among these were beings who had served the Savior during His mortal ministry. On 15 May 1829, the resurrected John the Baptist appeared to the Prophet and restored the authority of the Aaronic Priesthood (D&C 13).

There is an interesting entry in the Prophet's writings which seems to reflect upon this sacred experience. He said that the archangel Michael (Adam) had appeared "on the banks of the Susquehanna [River], detecting the devil when he appeared as an angel of light" (D&C 128:20). Concerning this matter, the author has written elsewhere: "Satan, aware of the magnitude of this event and its consequent power in curtailing his demoniacal domain, may have appeared to fabricate a false and powerless priesthood" (DCE, 17).

The adversary was ever mindful of the Prophet and of the events surrounding the restoration of the gospel to the earth. One of the Lord's latter-day witnesses, Elder Bruce R. McConkie, noted the following: "Such are the ways of Satan that when the God of heaven seeks to send the greatest light of the ages into the world, the forces of evil oppose it with the deepest darkness and iniquity of their benighted realm. Lucifer, our common enemy, fought the promised restoration as he now fights the accomplished restoration." (En, November 1975, p. 18.)

Harassed and Hounded by His Enemies

Despite the many difficulties he had to endure, Joseph the seer completed the translation of the sacred record in his possession and published it to the world in 1830. Within a matter of days after the Book of Mormon came off the press, Joseph Smith was commanded of God to organize anew the Church of Jesus Christ on earth. On 6 April 1830, having already been called of God as His prophet on earth, Joseph Smith was sustained by a small group of faithful followers as the first elder of the newly organized Church.

Shortly after the Church was organized, the Lord admonished His prophet to "be patient in afflictions, for thou shalt have many." However, He added these comforting words: "But endure them, for, lo, I am with thee, even unto the end of thy days." (D&C 24:8.) A little over a year earlier the Savior had intimated that Joseph's days might end in martyrdom (D&C 5:22).

The next years would be fraught with hardships for Joseph Smith. He would constantly be subjected to the ill will of those who failed to follow the One whose announced birth proclaimed "peace, good will toward men" (Luke 2:14).

The Prophet's family would also suffer from the unrelenting persecution heaped upon their husband and father. Joseph once said, "My family was kept in a continual state of alarm, not knowing, when I went from home, that I should ever return again; or what would befall me from day to day" (TS, 1:3).

One night in March 1832, while he was caring for an ill child, a mob broke into the home where he was staying and dragged the Prophet out into the cold. He was brutally beaten, resulting in severe back sprains from which he never fully recovered. An attempt was made to force both tar and an acidic poison into his mouth. In the process of resisting, one of Joseph's teeth was chipped. For over a decade thereafter, it was reported that the Prophet spoke with a slight lisp or whistlelike sound. His clothing was ripped from his body, and one of his assailants fell on him like a wild animal, cursing and scratching at his exposed flesh. The victim was then tarred and feathered and left half-unconscious and helpless on the cold, hard ground.

The Prophet essentially recovered from this frightful experience, but the infant he was caring for was not as fortunate. Joseph Murdock Smith, one of the twins the Prophet and his wife had adopted just eleven months earlier after the death of their own twins, died as a result of the exposure he received on that fateful night. In a later Church publication, this infant was referred to as "the first martyr of this dispensation." (MS 51:161.)

Joseph and others were once betrayed into the hands of a mob militia and sentenced to be shot. The courage of a Missouri state militia officer, Alexander W. Doniphan, prevented those demoniacal orders from being carried out.

The Prophet and five companions once spent more than four harsh winter months in a Missouri jail without benefit of heat, bedding, proper sanitation facilities, adequate ventilation, nutritious food, or any of the necessities and comforts that a civilized society should have provided prisoners—especially ones unjustly confined. Their darkened cell had but one small, heavily-barred window, and the room was only fourteen feet square with a seven-foot high ceiling. Their beds consisted of straw strewn on the uneven stone floor, or of roughly hewn logs. Their food often consisted of scraps from the jailer's table, and several times it was deliberately poisoned. For a period of five days, their captors tried to feed them on human flesh—"Mormon" beef, the jailers called it—but the prisoners refused to eat it. (HC 3:420.)

In the midst of these squalid conditions, the Prophet was often subjected to the vile and taunting ridicule of enemies whom the guards allowed to visit the jail. He and his brethren suffered spiritual and emotional distress as they heard reports of the widespread atrocities being committed against the scattered Saints who had been driven from their homes. Joseph's own wife had her house plundered by an apostate, leaving her with virtually nothing.

In these trying circumstances, feeling forgotten and forsaken, the Prophet cried out in anguish, "O God, where art thou?" After pouring out the pent up feelings of his pained soul, the suffering servant of the Almighty heard these words of comfort: "My son, peace be unto thy soul; thine adversity and thine afflictions shall be but a small moment; and then, if thou endure it well, God shall exalt thee on high; thou shalt triumph over all thy foes" (D&C 121:7–8).

In the most terrible physical surroundings, a sufferer's soul had been in tune with the Spirit, and God spoke words of comfort and counsel. What a magnificent lesson for any who find themselves in difficult circumstances!

The Lord spoke again to His prophet, reminding him of past trials and of sufferings that would *yet* have to be endured:

> If thou art called to pass through tribulation; if thou art in perils among false brethren; if thou art in perils among robbers; if thou art in perils by land or by sea;
>
> If thou art accused with all manner of false accusations; if thine enemies fall upon thee; if they tear thee from the society of thy father and mother and brethren and sisters; and if with a drawn sword thine enemies tear thee from the bosom of thy wife, and thine offspring, and thine elder son, although but six years of age, shall cling to thy garments, and shall say, My father, my father, why can't you stay with us? O, my father, what are the men going to do with you? and if then he shall be thrust from thee by the sword, and thou be dragged to prison, and thine enemies prowl around thee like wolves for the blood of the lamb;

And if thou shouldst be cast into the pit, or into the hands of murderers, and the sentence of death passed upon thee; if thou be cast into the deep; if the billowing surge conspire against thee; if fierce winds become thine enemy; if the heavens gather blackness, and all the elements combine to hedge up the way; and above all, if the very jaws of hell shall gape open the mouth wide after thee, know thou, my son, that all these things shall give thee experience, and shall be for thy good. (D&C 122:5-7.)

Then the Lord added this rebuking, but gentle, reminder: "The Son of Man hath descended below them all. Art thou greater than he?" (D&C 122:8.)

A great deal of time, effort, and valuable resources were expended in defending the Prophet in frivolous lawsuits. Brigham Young reported that "Joseph, our Prophet, was hunted and driven, arrested and persecuted, and although no law was ever made in these United States that would bear against him, for he never broke a law, yet to my certain knowledge he was defendant in forty-six lawsuits" (JD 14:199). On another occasion Brigham said that the number of lawsuits was forty-seven (JD 8:16).

On a few occasions, Joseph was actually convicted of the ludicrous charges levied against him. For example, he was found guilty of casting an evil spirit out of someone in New York. However, such an act was not against legal ordinances and statutes, and the Prophet was set free.

An evil enemy of both the Prophet and the Church was once successful in bringing an indictment against Joseph on charges of treason against the state of Missouri. A couple of maverick lawmen, one from Missouri and one from Carthage, Illinois, arrested the Prophet at a farm near Dixon, Illinois, some two hundred miles northeast of Nauvoo. They abused him so forcefully with their poking guns that Joseph's whole rib cage turned black and blue. The gunmen repeatedly threatened to shoot their hostage, who boldly bared his chest and said, " 'I am not afraid of your shooting; I am not afraid to die. . . . I have endured so much oppression, I am weary of life; and kill me, if you please. I am a strong man, however, and with my own natural weapons could soon level both of you; but if you have any legal process to serve, I

70

am at all times subject to law, and shall not offer resistance.' " (HC 5:440.)

The officers threatened to shoot one of Joseph's companions, Stephen Markham, who was then successful in obtaining a warrant for the arrest of the two men. An Illinois court released Joseph from their custody and also ruled that the indictment issued by Missouri was invalid.

Courageous in the Face of Adversity

Joseph Smith was always courageous in the face of danger. Just prior to his abduction in Dixon, having been warned of the possibility that some Missourians might try to capture him, the Prophet declared: "I have no fear. . . . I shall find friends, and Missourians cannot hurt me, I tell you in the name of the Lord." (ECH, 284.)

On another occasion a young man asked his prophet-leader, "Don't you get frightened when all those hounding wolves are after you?" Joseph replied, "No, I am not afraid; the Lord said he would protect me, and I have full confidence in His word." (YWJ 17:548.)

Once, while shackled in chains, Joseph was guarded by "the most noisy, foul-mouthed, vulgar, disgraceful rabble that ever defiled the earth," said one of his fellow prisoners, Parley P. Pratt. The captives endured a painful assault upon their hearts and ears as they were forced to listen "for hours to the obscene jests, the horrid oaths, the dreadful blasphemies and filthy language" of their guards. These vile men "even boasted of defiling by force wives, daughters and virgins, and of shooting or dashing out the brains of men, women and children."

Elder Pratt then described what happened as a prophet's cup of indignation was filled to overflowing:

> On a sudden he arose to his feet, and spoke in a voice of thunder, or as the roaring lion, uttering, as near as I can recollect, the following words:

71

"SILENCE, ye fiends of the infernal pit. In the name of Jesus Christ I rebuke you, and command you to be still; I will not live another minute and hear such language. Cease such talk, or you or I die THIS INSTANT!" He ceased to speak. He stood erect in terrible majesty. Chained, and without a weapon; calm, unruffled and dignified as an angel, he looked upon the quailing guards, whose weapons were lowered or dropped to the ground; whose knees smote together, and who, shrinking into a corner, or crouching at his feet, begged his pardon, and remained quiet till a change of guards.

I have seen the ministers of justice, clothed in magisterial robes, and criminals arraigned before them, while life was suspended on a breath, in the Courts of England; I have witnessed a Congress in solemn session to give laws to nations; I have tried to conceive of kings, of royal courts, of thrones and crowns; and of emperors assembled to decide the fate of kingdoms; but dignity and majesty have I seen but once, as it stood in chains, at midnight, in a dungeon in an obscure village of Missouri. (APP, 210–11.)

Prelude to Martyrdom: *The* Expositor *Wildfire*

Just as prophets and holy men who had preceded him, Joseph the Prophet would not always prevail over his enemies. The Lord had told him, "Thy days are known, and thy years shall not be numbered less" (D&C 122:9). There would come the day when his work would be completed and the protecting hand of the Lord would be withdrawn.

27 June 1844, was the day. Carthage, Illinois, was the place.

Clouds of darkness had been descending upon the Prophet for some weeks. False brethren and other enemies of the Church had plotted against, and had intensified their persecution of, the leaders of this latter-day faith.

The spark that seemed to ignite the explosion of gunfire that fateful day in Carthage occurred almost three weeks earlier. On Friday, 7 June, treacherous enemies of the Church published a newspaper in Nauvoo, Illinois, known as the Nauvoo *Expositor*.

Joseph Smith, as a mayor of the city, described the publication as a "foul, noisome, filthy sheet" (HC 6:585).

The citizens of Nauvoo had cause for concern. In the fourteen years the Church had existed, from 1830 to 1844, the Latter-day Saints had been driven from their homes many times by prejudice and persecution. They had finally settled as exiles in a swampy, malaria-infested piece of land on the banks of the Mississippi River and had transformed it into one of the most beautiful and prosperous cities in America. For a time they had enjoyed peace. That peace and their right to worship God according to the dictates of their own conscience were now threatened by a defamatory paper published in their midst.

The *Expositor* announced its purpose to become "the organ of the Reformed Mormon Church" and to seek the unconditional repeal of the Nauvoo City Charter. The charter was the legal document which guaranteed the citizens of Nauvoo broad protective powers from the prowling predators who were determined to destroy them. The paper maliciously slandered the prophet-mayor, calling him "one of the blackest and basest scoundrels that has appeared upon the stage of human existence since the days of Nero, and Caligula" (Nauvoo *Expositor*, June 7, 1844, p. 3).

Several days later, the city council, acting upon its legal charter, declared the newspaper a public nuisance and ordered the city marshal to destroy the press. This was done, they explained, "because of the libelous and slanderous character of the paper, its avowed intention being to destroy the municipality and drive the Saints from the city" (HC, 6:432). The city fathers considered the publication as a "stench, or putrified carcase [sic]" that should be removed (HC 6:585).

After the city marshal had dismantled the press and left the premises, the apostate owners set fire to their own building and fled to the nearby city of Carthage, where they claimed their lives had been threatened and their building burned. The fire was quickly discovered and put out by the citizens of Nauvoo. But the flames of hatred fanned by the enemies who had fled to Carthage turned into a far greater wildfire with tragic consequences.

The Warsaw *Signal*, a newspaper noted for its anti-Mormon sentiment, cried for the blood of the Saints: "We have only to state that this is sufficient! War and extermination is inevitable!

Citizens arise, One and All!!! Can you stand by, and suffer such Infernal Devils to rob men of their property and rights, without avenging them? We have no time to comment; every man will make his own. Let it be made with powder and ball!!!" The editor of the paper announced his readiness to cooperate in exterminating "the wicked and abominable Mormon leaders" (Warsaw *Signal*, June 19, 1844).

Mobs began to form in Carthage and Warsaw, and the following resolutions were passed:

> We hold ourselves at all times in readiness to co-operate with our fellow-citizens in this state, Missouri and Iowa, to exterminate, utterly exterminate the wicked and abominable Mormon leaders, the authors of our troubles. . . .
>
> Resolved, that the time, in our opinion, has arrived, when the adherents of Smith, as a body, should be driven from the surrounding settlements into Nauvoo. That the prophet and his miscreant adherents should then be demanded at their hands; and, if not surrendered, a war of extermination should be waged to the entire destruction, if necessary for our protection, of his adherents. (HC 6:464.)

The Saints sought help from the governor of the state, and the city council also submitted their case to two courts of law for trial regarding their actions. Both times the council was exonerated and set free. Such legal action did not satisfy Nauvoo's enemies. Governor Thomas Ford, who had come to Carthage and taken fellowship with the enemies of Joseph Smith, demanded that Joseph and other members of the council submit themselves to arrest and (illegally) be tried under the original warrant before an anti-Mormon magistrate in Carthage.

The prophet-mayor replied that he had already met the legal demands of the law and, furthermore, dared not go to Carthage and be tried before a prejudiced judge in the midst of his enemies. He added, "A burnt child dreads the fire."

Joseph and his brother Hyrum decided to leave Nauvoo and head west, feeling that if they were gone the hostilities would subside. The beleagured Joseph uttered these prophetic words: "I told Stephen Markham that if I and Hyrum were ever taken again we should be massacred, or I was not a prophet of God." (HC 6:546.)

After the two Smith brothers had left Nauvoo, the governor sent a posse to the city. They harassed and threatened the citizens. The governor's men demanded that the mayor and his brother return and submit themselves to arrest or the entire city would be placed under guard. Some of the fainthearted begged the Prophet to return, and Joseph replied, "If my life is of no value to my friends it is of none to myself." (HC 6:549.)

Resigned to their fate, Joseph and Hyrum sadly but resolutely returned to Nauvoo and prepared to submit themselves to arrest in Carthage. With a divine premonition that his life was fast coming to a close, the Prophet paused several times as he left Nauvoo to soak in the scenes of the city and people he loved so well. "This is the loveliest place and the best people under the heavens," he declared. "Little do they know the trials that await them." (HC 6:554.)

The Prophet further proclaimed: "I am going like a lamb to the slaughter; but I am calm as a summer's morning; I have a conscience void of offense towards God, and towards all men. I SHALL DIE INNOCENT, AND IT SHALL YET BE SAID OF ME — HE WAS MURDERED IN COLD BLOOD." (D&C 135:4.)

Upon arriving in Carthage, the prisoners were treated contemptuously by the wild mob that awaited them. Threatening to kill Joseph Smith, some of the riffraff yelled: "Clear the way and let us have a view of Joe Smith, the prophet of God. He has seen the last of Nauvoo. We'll use him up now, and kill all the damned Mormons." (HC 6:559.) The governor refused to meet with Mayor Smith and his companions, but he did address the hellbent horde that occupied the streets, promising them "full satisfaction."

In addition to the original charge of inciting a riot, the men from Nauvoo were additionally charged with treason against the state. Treason was considered a capital crime, and bail for such could only be fixed by a circuit judge, the nearest one being a day's ride away. Without a hearing, the hapless men were illegally confined to jail.

Joseph and Hyrum Smith, together with several other companions, spent the next two nights in Carthage Jail. Although he had promised them protection, there is ample evidence that Governor Ford was a man of little character; like another governor in another time—even Pontius Pilate—he had succumbed to the pressures of political expediency.

The prisoners were left to the fate which conspiring men had determined would befall them. Contrary to his promise to take the prophet-mayor with him if he went to Nauvoo on the morning of 27 June the governor left Carthage without the prisoners for a visit to the city of the Saints.

A melancholy mood settled upon the four men who remained in Carthage Jail. In addition to Joseph and Hyrum, there were Dr. Willard Richards and John Taylor, both members of the Council of the Twelve Apostles. Late in the afternoon the jailer suggested that the prisoners go into an inner cell for safety following supper. Joseph turned to Dr. Richards and said, " 'If we go into the cell, will you go in with us?' The doctor answered, 'Brother Joseph . . . you did not ask me to come to jail with you —and do you think I would forsake you now? But I will tell you what I will do; if you are condemned to be hung for treason, I will be hung in your stead, and you shall go free.' Joseph said, 'You cannot.' The doctor replied, 'I will.' " (HC 6:616.)

Innocent Blood Shed at Carthage

Shortly after this declaration of courageous allegiance to a beloved prophet, shouts and shots were heard from the street below. Glancing out of the window of their unbarred room on the second floor of the jail, Elder Richards saw a mob of about one hundred armed men with blackened faces crowding the jail door. The few guards made a token resistance, firing their weapons into the air but finally standing aside to allow the maddened mob to accomplish their diabolical work of death.

Shots were fired up the stairway leading to the room housing the prisoners, and simultaneously shots were fired through the open window from the outside. The rabble rushed up the stairs and began firing into the door that gave partial protection to the prisoners within. Gun barrels were then thrust through the small opening provided by the slightly ajar door and fired. These were defensively parried by canes in possession of the prisoners, who also pushed against the door to hold the brutes at bay. Joseph even had a small pistol which he discharged in the mob's direction.

Hyrum Smith, Patriarch to the Church, was shot with a bullet that struck him in the left side of his nose. He fell to the floor declaring, "I am a dead man!" "As he fell on the floor another ball from the outside entered his left side, and passed through his body with such force that it completely broke to pieces the watch he wore in his vest pocket, and at the same instant another ball from the door grazed his breast, and entered his head by the throat; subsequently a fourth ball entered his left leg." (HC 6:617.)

Looking upon his faithful and fallen brother, Joseph exclaimed, "Oh, dear Brother Hyrum."

John Taylor continued to parry the gun barrels with his cane but finally concluded that "resistance was vain, and he attempted to jump out of the window, where a ball fired from within struck him on his left thigh, hitting the bone, and passing through to within half an inch of the other side. He fell on the window sill, when a ball fired from the outside struck his watch in his vest pocket, and threw him back into the room.

"After he fell into the room he was hit by two more balls, one of them injuring his left wrist considerably, and the other entering at the side of the bone just below the left knee. He rolled under the bed, which was at the right of the window in the south-east corner of the room." As his bleeding body lay there, bullets continued to be fired at him, one of which tore a large piece of flesh from his left hip. (HC 6:618.)

"Joseph, seeing there was no safety in the room, and no doubt thinking that it would save the lives of his brethren in the room if he could get out, turned calmly from the door, dropped his pistol on the floor, and sprang into the window when two balls pierced him from the door, and one entered his right breast from without, and he fell outward into the hands of his murderers, exclaiming, 'O Lord, my God!' " (HC 6:618.)

There is no universal agreement as to whether the Prophet was dead when he hit the ground. Some say he lived long enough to pull himself up against a well outside the jail. There was, however, no molestation of his lifeless body, which later examination revealed had four bullet wounds in it.

Dallin H. Oaks and Marvin S. Hill have written: "The murder of Joseph and Hyrum Smith at Carthage, Illinois, was not a spontaneous, impulsive act by a few personal enemies of the Mormon leaders, but a deliberate political assassination, committed or condoned by some of the leading citizens in Hancock County" (CC, 6).

John Taylor survived his terrible wounds to later become the third prophet and President of The Church of Jesus Christ of Latter-day Saints. He would yet suffer greatly and, in a sense, at his death be considered a martyr, as we shall later see. Willard Richards miraculously survived the attack with nothing but a minor bullet graze on the lower part of his left ear. "His escape fulfilled literally a prophecy which Joseph made over a year previously, that the time would come that the balls would fly around him like hail, and he should see his friends fall on the right and on the left, but that there should not be a hole in his garment." (HC 6:619.)

Writing of the martyrdom of Joseph Smith the Prophet and Hyrum Smith the Patriarch, John Taylor declared, "The testators are now dead, and their testament is in force" (D&C 135:5). "The sealing of the testimony through the shedding of blood would not have been complete in the death of the Prophet Joseph Smith alone," affirmed President Joseph Fielding Smith. "It required the death of Hyrum Smith who jointly held the keys of this dispensation. It was needful that these martyrs seal their testimony with their blood, that they 'might be honored and the wicked might be condemned." (DS 1:219; see also D&C 136:39.)

Reactions to the Martyrdoms

The Saints were stricken with grief at the deaths of their beloved leaders. The city of Nauvoo, and Mormons everywhere, mourned their loss. Yet, in death there was a sense of triumph.

Lucy Mack Smith, the grieving mother, reported the following as she gazed upon the lifeless bodies of her noble sons: "I seemed almost to hear them say, 'Mother, weep not for us, we have overcome the world by love; we carried to them the gospel, that their souls might be saved; they slew us for our testimony, and thus placed us beyond their power; their ascendency is for a moment, ours is an eternal triumph.'

"I then thought upon the promise which I had received in Missouri, that in five years Joseph should have power over all his enemies. The time had elapsed and the promise was fulfilled." (HJS, 325.)

From the poetic pen of Eliza R. Snow came these comforting words:

> Now Zion mourns—she mourns an earthly head:
> The Prophet and the Patriarch are dead!
> The blackest deed that men or devils know,
> Since Calv'ry's scene, has laid the brothers low!
> One in their life, and one in death—they prov'd
> How strong their friendship—how they truly lov'd:
> True to their mission, until death, they stood,
> Then seal'd their testimony with their blood.
> All hearts with sorrow bleed, and ev'ry eye
> Is bath'd in tears—each bosom heaves a sigh—
> Heartbroken widows' agonizing groans
> Are mingled with the helpless orphans' moans!
> Ye Saints! be still, and know that God is just—
> With steadfast purpose in his promise trust:
> Girded with sackcloth, own his mighty hand,
> And wait his judgments on this guilty land!
> The noble martyrs now have gone to move
> The cause of Zion in the courts above.
> (TS, 5:575.)

The enemies of Joseph Smith and the divine work he was called to direct fiendishly exulted over his death. With one exception, their comments are not worth repeating. That exception is the false prophecy made by the New York *Herald,* which boldly proclaimed in its 7–8 July 1844 edition: "Thus Ends Mormonism!" The paper further stated that "the 'latter day saints' have indeed come to the latter day" (CN, Jan. 11, 1975, C-16).

Some Concluding Thoughts to Ponder

When Moroni first appeared to Joseph Smith on the night of 21 September 1823, he said Joseph's "name should be had for good and evil among all nations, kindreds, and tongues, or that it should be both good and evil spoken of among all people" (Joseph Smith—History 1:33). The truth of this statement would come vividly to his mind during the ensuing experiences that ultimately led to his martyrdom twenty-one years later.

Although it has been many years since his death, the name of Joseph Smith still evokes strong feelings among the peoples of the earth. While millions revere him as a true prophet of God, his detractors use every possible ploy to discredit and malign the man whose work will have an eternal bearing on their salvation.

Two significant statements by other modern-day prophets give us some insights on the relationship of the Prophet Joseph Smith to those who faithfully follow him and to those who foolishly reject him:

First, a thought from President Joseph Fielding Smith:

> If Joseph Smith was verily a prophet, and if he told the truth when he said that he stood in the presence of angels sent from the Lord, and obtained keys of authority, and the commandment to organize the Church of Jesus Christ once again on the earth, then this knowledge is of the most vital importance to the entire world. *No man can reject that testimony without incurring the most dreadful consequences, for he cannot enter the kingdom of God.* It is, therefore, *the duty of every man to investigate* that he may weigh this matter carefully and know the truth. (DS 1:189–90.)

Second, this observation from President George Albert Smith:

> There have been some who have belittled [Joseph Smith], but I would like to say that those who have done so will be

80

forgotten and their remains will go back to mother earth, if they have not already gone, and the odor of their infamy will never die, while the glory and honor and majesty and courage and fidelity manifested by the Prophet Joseph Smith will attach to his name forever (CR, April 1946, pp. 181–82).

CHAPTER SIX

Persecution of a New Faith

Suffering of the Smith Family

Joseph Smith's claims to heavenly manifestations and divine powers had the effect of kindling fires of hostility and hatred in the hearts of many misguided men and women. The flames of persecution were not directed at the young prophet alone but reached out to engulf any who followed or expressed a belief in Joseph's mission and message. This seemed particularly true for the Prophet's family, who were frequently forced to flee the comforts of home and seek shelter and safety in new locations.

They were constantly subjected to ridicule and the abuse of lying tongues. Recalling some of these circumstances, the Prophet said: "Rumor with her thousand tongues was all the time employed in circulating falsehoods about my father's family, and about myself. If I were to relate a thousandth part of them, it would fill up volumes." (HC 1:19.)

Even Joseph's older brother Alvin, who had passed away in 1823, was the object of a vile rumor that caused the family considerable distress. The story was circulated that his father had allowed his son's body to be dug up and dissected. To finally put the rumor to rest, the father helped exhume Alvin's body to prove the story was false.

Joseph Smith, Sr., was once offered the choice of having a fourteen-dollar debt forgiven if he would "burn up those Books of

Mormon" or of going to jail. He chose the latter rather than to deny or desecrate that which he knew to be true. Years later this faithful man died from an illness contracted from exposure to the elements after being driven from his Missouri home.

Along with other members of the family, the Prophet's younger brother, Samuel H. Smith, suffered greatly for his testimony of the Savior and the divine work of his prophet-brother. "On the day a malicious mob murdered his brothers, Joseph and Hyrum, Samuel was relentlessly pursued by a contingent of that mob. Because of the severe fatigue brought on by that chase, a fever was contracted which, according to John Taylor, 'laid the foundation for his death, which took place on the 30th of July, [1844].' " (DCE, 536.) Thus, although not felled by bullet or blade, Samuel might also be considered a martyr to the cause of Christ.

As mentioned in the previous chapter, one of the Prophet Joseph's adopted children, Joseph Murdock Smith, died as a result of exposure which occurred the night the Prophet was viciously abducted from his home, beaten, tarred, and feathered. The trauma of this night of terror undoubtedly left deep scars on Joseph's wife, Emma. She knew little peace during her married life with her persecuted prophet-husband.

Opposition to the Newly Organized Church

The persecution suffered by Joseph Smith and his small circle of family and friends during the decade of 1820–1830 intensified and expanded following the organization of The Church of Jesus Christ of Latter-day Saints on 6 April 1830 in Fayette, New York. As proselyting activities commenced and converts began to gather to the newly organized Church—not a *new* church but a *restoration* of the original Church established by Jesus Christ—opposition to the Prophet and his followers increased.

Within several months after the Church was organized, a mob tore down a dam which the Saints had built across a stream in Colesville, New York, for the purpose of baptizing. The dam was repaired, and thirteen people were baptized, much to the displeasure of about fifty detractors that gathered shortly thereafter and began to threaten and insult the small group of believers. That evening a meeting of the Saints was disrupted and Joseph Smith was arrested on charges of being "a disorderly person, setting the country in an uproar by preaching the Book of Mormon" (ECH, 85).

Joseph's affable personality and integrity of character soon won the heart of the constable who arrested him. The officer informed the Prophet that a mob was waiting to waylay him as they traveled to the place of trial. Instead of abetting the mob, the constable protected the Prophet.

By December 1830, the Lord had told the Church to move to Ohio (D&C 37:3). This revelation was followed on 2 January 1831 with the warning that the Saints were to go to Ohio to "escape the power of the enemy, and be gathered unto me a righteous people" (D&C 38:31).

The Church in Ohio:
Peace and Persecution

"From within her borders, Ohio was to give birth to the fundamental organization that exists within the Church today. The First Presidency of the Church was established in Ohio, as well as the Quorum of the Twelve Apostles, . . . Quorum of the Seventy, and the first stake of the Church, with its attendant high council. Between February 1831 and April 1836, sixty-four of the revelations recorded in the Doctrine and Covenants were received in Ohio." (DCE, 393.) In addition, the first latter-day temple was built and important priesthood keys of authority were restored within its walls following a personal visit by Him whose house it was, even the Savior.

Peace was not to prevail, however, as persecution was renewed. Some citizens of Ohio began to be alarmed at the influx of Latter-day Saints in their state. Joseph reported that by the spring of 1831 "many false reports, lies, and foolish stories, were published in the newspapers, and circulated in every direction, to prevent people from investigating the work, or embracing the faith" (HC 1:158). About a year later the infant Joseph Murdock

84

Smith lost his life several days after the beating of the Prophet. Sidney Rigdon was also beaten into unconsciousness on that fateful night.

A Missionary Martyr

A great deal of opposition was directed towards the missionaries who went forth to spread the word. Just like their prophet-leader, many were dragged into courts of law and falsely charged with a wide range of accusations. Some were pelted with eggs and rocks, while others suffered beatings. Their experience was not unlike that of the messengers sent forth to preach the word of the Lord in ancient times.

The earliest reported killing of a missionary was that of Elder Joseph B. Brackenbury in Pomfret, New York, on 7 January 1832. Andrew Jenson reported that Elder Brackenbury died "from the effects of poison administered by his enemies. The doctors attempted to dig him up to use his body as a subject for dissection, but were hindered in their intentions by Elder Joel H. Johnson, who was warned in a dream of the matter in progress, and rose from his bed at 11 o'clock at night. Together with his brother David he went to the grave and succeeded in arresting one of the parties while at work with a spade and a hand sledge." (LDSBE, 2:597.)

Since that first death, hundreds of missionaries have lost their lives in the mission field while serving in the cause of Christ.

Troubles in Missouri

Although the headquarters of the Church remained in Ohio until the late 1830s, another center for the gathering Saints was established in western Missouri, which at that time was the frontier of the United States. On 7 June 1831, the Lord revealed this location as "the land which I will consecrate unto my people, . . . the land of your inheritance" (D&C 52:2–5). Later, the city of Independence, Jackson County, Missouri, was specifically identified as the "place for the city of Zion" which the Latter-day Saints were to establish (D&C 57:1–4).

The Latter-day Saints were not readily accepted by the older settlers. For one thing, Missouri had been admitted to the Union as a slave state, and the natives were suspicious of these new residents from the North. The old settlers were comfortable with their life-style, which was threatened by the large influx of strangers who proclaimed this land to be their new Zion.

B. H. Roberts reported that "as early as the spring of 1832 there began to appear signs of an approaching storm. In the deadly hours of the night the houses of some of the saints were stoned, the windows broken, and the inmates disturbed. In the fall of the same year a large quantity of hay in the stack belonging to the saints was burned, houses shot into, and the people insulted with abusive language." (MP, 73.)

In the spring of 1833, Reverend Finis Ewing, head of a local church, published a tirade against the Saints that included this inflamatory statement: "The Mormons are the common enemies of mankind, and ought to be destroyed" (HC 1:392).

By July, there were over twelve hundred Latter-day Saints in Jackson County, one-third of the county's population. Seeing their majority rapidly dwindling, the older citizens took action. A document known as the "Secret Constitution" was circulated among enemies of the Church that, among other things, called for the removal of Church members from Jackson County.

On 20 July a committee of old settlers presented to a few of the leaders of the Church in Missouri their demands for the immediate removal of the Saints. Church leaders asked for three months in which to consider the proposition, which would give them time to counsel with the authorities in Ohio. Besides, closing their printing office and moving the large body of members would require some time. This being denied, they asked for ten days, but were given only fifteen minutes in which to make their decision.

Shortly thereafter, a mob broke into the printing office and home of W. W. Phelps, which housed the Church printing press. Mrs. Phelps, with a sick infant in her arms, and the rest of her children were forced out of the home, which the mob then proceeded to demolish. The intruders threw the printing press from a second-story window, threw furniture into the street, tore the roof off the structure, and tore down the walls.

Other buildings were attacked, and two of the leading elders of the Church, Charles Allen and Bishop Edward Partridge, were dragged "through the maddened crowd, which insulted and abused them along the road to the public square. Here two alternatives were presented them: either they must renounce their faith in the Book of Mormon, or leave the county." (MP, 85.)

The men refused to do either; Bishop Partridge told the mob that Saints in all ages had been persecuted, and he was willing to suffer for the sake of Christ. His words were soon drowned by the tumult of the angry crowd, whose vile oaths and wicked expressions "were enough to put hell itself to shame. The two brethren, Partridge and Allen, were stripped of their outer clothing, and daubed with tar, mixed with lime or pearl-ash, or some other flesh-eating acid, and a quantity of feathers scattered over them." (MP, 86.)

Blood is Shed

Several days later, like a pack of vicious animals that had tasted blood and wanted more, a mob returned to Independence looking for more victims. Their threats included the following: "We will rid Jackson County of the 'Mormons,' peaceably if we can, forcibly if we must. If they will not go without, we will whip and kill the men; we will destroy their children, *and ravish their women.*" (MP, 88.)

Outrages against the Latter-day Saints continued in the weeks and months ahead. The Church members sought redress through the courts but were also preparing to defend themselves if necessary. On the night of 31 October 1833, about forty or fifty men rode into what was known as the Whitmer settlement, located west of the Big Blue River not far from Independence. They pulled the roofs off from about a dozen homes and severely whipped some of the men. The following night an attack on another settlement was prevented because two "spies" from the mob were caught and detained. However, some homes in Independence were broken into, and the Church store of Gilbert, Whitney, and Company was ransacked.

One of those who broke into the store was apprehended in the act and taken before a justice of the peace. The justice, an obvious sympathizer of the anti-Mormon mob activities, refused to accept the charges against the intruder and released the prisoner. Several days later this same man went before the same justice and obtained a warrant for the arrest of those who had caught him breaking into the store, charging them with "assault and battery" and "false imprisonment." One of those so falsely accused ironically commented, "Although we could not obtain a warrant against him for breaking open the store, yet he had gotten one for us, for catching him at it." (MP, 103.)

Mob activity continued the night of 2 November, when a house located on the Big Blue was unroofed and a sick man by the name of David Bennet was assaulted. After beating the defenseless man, his assailants shot him. However, rather than entering his skull, the ball cut a deep gash across the top of his head.

Two days later about forty mob members took over a Mormon-owned ferry boat on the Big Blue River and drove the owners away with threats of violence. Property was destroyed and some Church members were chased and threatened. When other Latter-day Saints came to the rescue, a gun battle ensued. Two mob members were killed in the fray, including one who had boasted that "with ten fellows I will wade to my knees in blood, but what I will drive the 'Mormons' from Jackson County." (MP, 102.)

Church member Philo Dibble was seriously wounded, being shot in the bowels. He had a miraculous recovery from his wounds, following a priesthood blessing, and lived to later cross the plains with the Saints and settle in Utah, where he died in 1895 (MP, 102).

A young Church member named Andrew Barber was not as fortunate. He was mortally wounded in the battle. It is reported that some of the brethren wanted to administer to him, but young Barber, perhaps knowing that his mission in life was complete, stopped them. He reported seeing angels in the room and passed peacefully from life the day following the battle at the Big

Blue. He thus became the first Latter-day Saint martyr to lose his life by the shedding of blood.

Zion's Camp

One and one-half months following the death of Andrew Barber at the Big Blue, the Prophet Joseph Smith received a revelation in which a parable was given regarding "the redemption of Zion" (D&C 101:43; see verses 43–62). Its message may have been veiled to outsiders, but it was clear to the seer of the Lord —gather together the necessary forces and march to the defense of the beleagured Saints in Missouri.

On 24 February 1834, the Prophet received a rather specific revelation regarding the redemption of Zion. The Lord commanded that a force of men be organized to "go up unto the land of Zion, by tens, or by twenties, or by fifties, or by an hundred, until they have obtained to the number of five hundred of the strength of my house." He went on to say that if this many could not be found, the minimum number of men for the expedition should be one hundred. (D&C 103:30–34.)

This band of men came to be known as Zion's Camp. It took the leaders of the Church about two and one-half months to recruit the necessary manpower. A small group of volunteers left Kirtland, Ohio, on 1 May 1834 and proceeded to a rendezvous point to await the others. The camp eventually consisted of 207 men, 11 women, and 11 children. The oldest among them was a man named Samuel Baker, who was almost eighty, and there were two sixteen-year-olds among them. (HR, 181, 185, 416.)

In about a month and one-half, the members of Zion's Camp walked over one thousand miles from Ohio to Missouri. Their journey took them from the northeastern part of Ohio, through the states of Indiana and Illinois, and on to the western borders of Missouri, where Jackson County was located. Many of the men had left home with faith in the rightness of the cause they had embraced, but with a fear of the unknown and wondering if they would ever see their families again in mortality.

The journey proved to be a refining process. Obedience, faith, patience, and charity were not the least of the traits that needed to be finely honed along the way as the men struggled with many physical hardships and spiritual challenges. As in all ages when the Lord has asked an "army of Israel" to march, there were those who murmured. George A. Smith noted that "even a dog could not bark at some men without their murmuring at Joseph" (HR, 188).

On 3 June the Prophet stood on the back of a wagon, admonishing and prophesying. Heber C. Kimball reported what transpired: "He said the Lord had told him that there would be a scourge come upon the camp, in consequence of the fractious and unruly spirits that appeared among them and they should die like sheep with the rot; still if they would repent and humble themselves before the Lord, the scourge in a great measure might be turned away; but, as the Lord lives, this camp will suffer for giving way to their unruly temper" (TS 6:788).

The prophesied plague smote the camp in the form of a dreaded disease—cholera. The disease struck with such force that men suddenly fell to the ground as if they had been shot. Before the scourge had run its course, about seventy people had been stricken, and thirteen had lost their lives. Those who died were John S. Carter, Eber Wilcox, Seth Hitchcock, Erastus Rudd, Alfred Risk, Edward Ives, Noah Johnson, Jesse B. Lawson, Robert McCord, Elial Strong, Jesse Smith, Warren Ingalls, and Betsy Parrish. (HR, 194, 417.)

While it is true that some of these may have died in Uzza-like fashion—stricken for trying to "steady the ark" (1 Chronicles 13:9–10) by complaining against the Prophet or God Himself—the fact remains that each had come on the march voluntarily. Each came at great sacrifice in response to a call to serve God and the suffering Saints in Missouri. Could they not be considered martyrs to the cause of Christ? The Eternal Judge will make that determination.

On 8 February 1835, the Prophet Joseph informed Brigham and Joseph Young of a vision he had received that gives additional insight on this matter. Said he: "Brethren, I have seen those men who died of the cholera in our camp; and the Lord knows, if I get a mansion as bright as theirs, I ask no more." Then the Prophet commenced to weep and for some time was unable to speak. (HC 2:181n.)

90

Upon arriving at their destination, the members of the camp were disheartened to learn that the governor of Missouri had backed away from an earlier promise of help in restoring the Saints to their rightful properties. Furthermore, he directly contradicted an earlier communique and announced that the Mormons had "no right to march to Jackson county in arms" (HC 2:86).

The Prophet informed the camp that their sacrifice had been sufficient and they would not be called upon to fight. On 22 June the Lord revealed that the redemption of Zion would be delayed "for a little season" (D&C 105:9). Because of their failure to restore the Saints to their homes, some felt the march had been a failure. However, Zion's Camp had succeeded in bringing some supplies to the oppressed Saints in Missouri, and they had been through a refining process that prepared many of them for greater service in the kingdom of God. Elder Neal A. Maxwell noted: "God is more concerned with growth than with geography. Thus, those who marched in Zion's Camp were not exploring the Missouri countryside but their own possibilities." (CR, October 1976, p. 16.)

One of the participants, Wilford Woodruff, who later became an Apostle and then prophet of the Lord, said the following of his experience with Zion's Camp: "We accomplished a great deal, though apostates and unbelievers many times asked the question, 'What have you done?' We gained an experience that we never could have gained in any other way. We had the privilege of beholding the face of the prophet and we had the privilege of traveling a thousand miles with him, and seeing the workings of the Spirit of God with him, and the revelations of Jesus Christ unto him and the fulfilment of those revelations. . . . Had I not gone up with Zion's Camp I should not have been here to-day." (JD 13:158.)

The Siege of DeWitt

The Saints were forced to flee Jackson County and subsequently were hounded from within the borders of Clay County, although much more peacefully. By the summer of 1838 there were

91

over fifteen thousand Latter-day Saints estimated in northern Missouri. Their growing numbers were a threat to many of the old settlers, particularly in the political arena. On 6 August 1838, a fight broke out at the polls in Gallatin when a group tried to prevent some Mormon men from voting. Soon armed mobs began threatening Mormon settlements.

The Mormon settlement of DeWitt was placed under siege by an armed mob on 21 September 1838. Livestock was driven off, and the besieged populace was forced to live off its rapidly diminishing provisions. On the twenty-first day of this harassment, the Saints finally agreed to vacate their town with the understanding that they would be compensated for the loss of their property (which never happened).

On the afternoon of 11 October, the exiles left their homes, "destitute, hungry and cold. They were emaciated by their long siege; many had died from this abuse; several more died on the march to Far West, a distance of fifty miles." (ECH, 222.) The deaths brought about by empty bellies and exposure were just as real as if guns had been placed at the victims' heads and the triggers pulled. In this sense, these Saints who died were just as much martyrs as they would have been had a direct act of violence been committed against them.

The mob's success at DeWitt added fuel to the fires of prejudice, violence, and hatred against the Latter-day Saints. Homes were burned and the inhabitants were driven out into the snowy October weather. The plight of Agnes M. Smith, whose husband Don Carlos was away from home on a mission, was typical of many. She was forced to wade through the cold waters of the Grand River with two small children as she fled the mobbers.

The Battle of Crooked River

In addressing the Church members on Sunday, 14 October 1838, Joseph Smith cited these memorable words of the One who best knew their meaning: "Greater love hath no man than this, that a man lay down his life for his friends" (John 15:13). One wonders if the Prophet had a foreboding premonition regarding the tragic events that would take place within the next two weeks. And could he have reflected upon a conversation he had with David W. Patten some six months earlier? On that occasion, Elder Patten "made known to the Prophet that he had asked the Lord to let him die the death of a martyr." The Prophet's response was, "When a man of your faith asks the Lord for anything he generally gets it." (LDP, 58.)

Such a request may seem out of order unless one considers the probability of divine promptings. Could the Lord have revealed this possibility to David, along with the question, "Would you be willing to die for My sake?"

The great prophet Nephi, who lived at the time the Savior was born into this world, was once promised that "all things shall be done unto thee according to thy word, for thou shalt not ask that which is contrary to my will" (Helaman 10:5). It is reasonable to believe that the same promise applied to a latter-day Apostle and man of faith, even David W. Patten.

In any event, Elder Patten's wish was not long in being granted. On 24 October 1838, an armed mob threatened to give the Mormons in Far West "hell" before noon the next day. Three men were kidnapped by the ruffians, who threatened to kill them. A county judge authorized a company of militia to disperse the mob and retake the prisoners.

About midnight the trumpet sounded in the town square of Far West as volunteers were sought to go to the rescue of the captives. David Patten, a captain in the state militia, responded to the call and was given command of a company of men. They then proceeded to a spot about fifteen miles south of Far West, where the mobbers were encamped with their prisoners in a bend of Crooked River.

The militia hoped to surprise the mobbers and avoid bloodshed. Early on the morning of 25 October, the group of rescuers arrived at their destination and proceeded to look for the encampment. The silhouettes of the Mormon militia were easily seen as the dawning light began to appear. A shot rang out and "young Patrick O'Bannion reeled out of the ranks and fell mortally wounded." With the watchword of "God and Liberty" impressed on their minds, the militia charged forward at Captain Patten's command. After exchanging gunfire, close sword combat took place. The mob finally took flight, but one mobber "wheeled, and shot Captain Patten, who instantly fell, mortally wounded."

David Patten lived long enough to bear his dying testimony to his wife. "Beloved," he said, "whatever you do else, do not deny the faith." He followed this appeal with a short prayer and then breathed his last mortal breath.

On the day of Elder Patten's funeral, the Prophet pointed at the lifeless body and said, "There lies a man that has done just as he said he would—he has laid down his life for his friends." (HC 3:175.)

One need not wonder how the Lord felt about this noble servant. In a revelation given in January 1841, the Savior said, "David Patten I have taken unto myself" (D&C 124:130).

One other Latter-day Saint lost his life in addition to Patrick O'Bannion and David Patten. Gideon Carter was shot in the face, which was so brutally shattered that none immediately recognized him. His body was retrieved when it was discovered who he was. Seven others were wounded, including James Hendricks, who was shot in the neck and paralyzed from the neck down. Following a priesthood blessing he was able to recover sufficiently that he later went west with the Saints and became a bishop of a Salt Lake City congregation.

The Haun's Mill Massacre

Two days after the deaths of the martyrs at Crooked River, the infamous extermination order was issued by the mob-sympathizing governor of Missouri, Lilburn W. Boggs. "The Mormons must be treated as enemies," he said, "and *must be exterminated* or driven from the state" (HC 3:175).

This "license to kill Latter-day Saints" was quickly acted upon. On 30 October 1838, an armed mob of 240 men swooped down on the tiny Mormon community of Haun's Mill and wantonly began to carry out Boggs' extermination order. The attack came without warning, only two days after the mobs had signed a peace treaty with the peaceful citizens of that settlement.

94

A cry of "peace" went unheeded as the mobbers indiscriminately opened fire on men, women, and children. Those who sought refuge in the blacksmith shop found themselves open targets as guns were discharged at them through the wide cracks between the logs. Before the massacre was over, according to the mob's own bragging, over sixteen hundred shots had been fired at the few inhabitants of this small settlement.

Acts of savagery were common among these hate-filled demons in human form. One fiend found ten-year-old Sardius Smith hiding under the bellows in the blacksmith shop. He dragged the boy out, "placed the muzzle of his gun near the boy's head and literally shot off the top of it." (MP, 235.)

The wicked wretch afterwards "described, with fiendish glee, how the poor boy struggled in his dying agony, and justified his savage and inhuman conduct in killing a mere child by saying, 'Nits will make lice, and if he had lived he would have been a Mormon' " (ECH, 196).

The pleas for mercy of an old veteran of the revolutionary war, Thomas McBride, were ignored—he was shot with the gun he had surrendered. One of the monsters then proceeded to hack the dying man's body "with a rude sword, or corn knife, until it was frightfully mangled." (ECH, 195–96.) Boots and other articles of clothing were pulled off the dead and dying, and then the homes were looted and ransacked.

The massacre left seventeen martyrs dead or dying, and the butchers rode off boasting of their deeds of brutality. Cain, too, gloried momentarily in his infamous deed of death (Moses 5:31–33). But just as he paid a terrible price for the murder of Abel, so too will those responsible for the massacre of the innocent at Haun's Mill have a price to pay for their diabolical deeds.

"The names of those killed are as follows: Thomas McBride, Levi N. Merrick, Elias Benner, Josiah Fuller, Benjamin Lewis, Alexander Campbell, Warren Smith, George S. Richards, William Napier, Austin Hammer, Simeon Cox, Hiram Abbott, John York, John Lee, John Byers, Sardius Smith and Charles Merrick. Some of these were mere children. Many others were severely wounded but managed to escape with their lives, among them a boy, Alma Smith, who had the flesh of his hip shot away. He had the presence of mind to lie perfectly still and the fiends thought he was dead. Alma was miraculously healed through prayer and faith." (ECH, 196.)

Young Alma's recovery is a remarkable story of faith and inspiration on the part of his now widowed mother, Amanda Smith. Throughout the night this grieving mother prayed for help regarding her suffering son. The answers to her fervent prayers came with great clarity. "I was directed as by a voice speaking to me," she said.

She was directed to pack the boy's wound with a lye made from the ashes of the shag-bark hickory they had burned earlier. She was then inspired to "make a slippery-elm poultice and fill the wound with it." Her testimony was that she was "instructed as distinctly as though a physician had been standing by speaking to me."

Full of faith she told her boy that "the Lord can make something there in the place of your hip." The healing took place as the boy "laid on his face for five weeks, until he was entirely recovered—a flexible gristle having grown in place of the missing joint and socket." According to this faithful woman, the boy was never "the least crippled during his life" and was "a living miracle of the power of God." (WM, 124, 128.)

The Haun's Mill massacre was the last of the savage acts of bloodshed committed against the Saints in Missouri. Others would yet suffer death and depravation as a result of being cruelly driven from the comfort and safety of their homes. "It is estimated that not less than three hundred of the Saints lost their lives from these causes in the Missouri persecutions alone." (MS 51:161.)

The persecutions and martyrdoms that took place in Missouri would not be the last the Saints would see. More trials were yet to follow and more of the faithful would fall by the hands of assassins.

CHAPTER SEVEN

Persecution and Pioneers

The Founding of Nauvoo

In January 1839, the exiled Saints began leaving the troubled land of Missouri, finding refuge in western Illinois. They soon settled in a swampy, mosquito-infested place on the banks of the Mississippi River known as Commerce. Much property was purchased with promissory notes, and the new citizens began in earnest to create their city beautiful—Nauvoo.

Swamp land was drained and brush cut away, and soon beautiful homes replaced ramshackle huts. The combination of faith and hard work created a city that by 1841 became the most populous in the state of Illinois. A charter was granted by the state legislature that granted the citizens of Nauvoo broad powers designed to protect them from many of the abuses they had previously suffered.

A season of relative peace rested upon them in spite of the efforts of outside agitators to bring trouble to their doorsteps.

Hostilities Continue in Illinois

Mob members from Missouri, not satisfied with having driven the Latter-day Saints from their state, crossed the border into Illinois to foment trouble. On 7 July 1840, marauders from Missouri kidnapped four Mormon men and forced them across the state line, taking them to a small town called Tully. One of the prisoners, Benjamin Boyce,

> was stripped and tied to a tree and whipped with gads until his body was mangled from his shoulders to his knees. In the meantime [Alanson] Brown had been hung by the neck until life appeared to be gone, then the ruffians cut him down, revived him, and returned to Tully with them both. They then placed ropes on the necks of [James] Allred and [Noah] Rogers and took them out to the woods, where they stripped them of their clothing and made many threats against their lives. Rogers was badly beaten, as Boyce had been, but for some reason the fiends refrained from whipping Allred. (ECH, 299.)

Allred and Brown were released by the brutes almost a week after their kidnapping, and Allred was given an affidavit stating there was "nothing to justify his detention any longer" (HC 4:157). Boyce and Rogers remained prisoners in chains until 21 August, when they escaped.

During the next four years, until the martyrdoms of Joseph and Hyrum Smith on 27 June 1844, many of the hostile actions taken against the Latter-day Saints took place on legal battlegrounds. The Prophet continued to be hounded by enemies who tried multiple legal ruses to deprive him of his liberties.

Hostilities Following the Martyrdoms of Joseph and Hyrum

Enemies of The Church of Jesus Christ of Latter-day Saints were dismayed to discover that the deaths of Joseph and Hyrum Smith did not destroy the Church. Under the leadership of the Twelve Apostles, the work went forward. The opposition increased its political clout sufficiently so that in January 1845 the Nauvoo Charter was repealed by the state legislature. This left the citizens of the "City Beautiful" without legal government and without the protection it had previously enjoyed from outside agitators.

98

During the summer of 1845 several anti-Mormon newspapers began to incite opposition to the Church and its members. Acts of vandalism against the Latter-day Saints were renewed, and by September some homes had been burned and their occupants driven from their property. When non-Mormon Sheriff J. B. Backenstos tried to quell mob violence, he himself was driven from his home, threatened by the mob, and finally arrested on charges of killing a mob member. A mass meeting held in Quincy, Illinois, called for the removal of the Latter-day Saints from the state "as speedily as possible."

Brigham Young, the President of the Council of the Twelve Apostles, replied that it was the intention of Church members to leave Illinois the following spring. This would give the Saints sufficient time to properly dispose of their property and to prepare for their journey to "some point so remote that there will not need to be any difficulty with the people and ourselves." (ECH, 326.)

On 2 October 1845, an anti-Mormon convention was held in Carthage. Those opposed to the Latter-day Saints agreed to "accept the proposition made by the Mormons to remove from the State next spring and to wait with patience the time for removal" (RC, 216).

Patience was among the many other virtues the mobocrats lacked, and they did not wait until spring to renew their acts of violence and vandalism against the Saints. During this time Edmund Durfee was killed by a mob in Hancock County and Joshua Smith was poisoned in Carthage (MS 51:162).

The Exodus from Nauvoo

Hostilities increased to the point that in order to prevent bloodshed the exodus was moved ahead. The first wagons to leave Nauvoo were ferried across the cold Mississippi River on 4 February 1846. A temporary camp was set up about nine miles from the river in a place called Sugar Creek. Others soon followed as the Saints left the warmth of their comfortable homes in Illinois and set up housekeeping in tents and wagons on the snowy soil of Iowa. By the twenty-fifth of the month the weather was so cold that at least one man walked across the river on a solid sheet of ice. The following day, wagons drove over the hardened icy highway.

One of the exiles described their situation as follows: "By the first of March over five thousand exiles were shivering behind the meager shelter of wagon covers and tents, and the winter-stripped groves that lined the creek. Their sufferings have never been adequately told; and to realize how cruel and ill-timed was this forced exodus, one has only to be reminded that in one night nine children were born under these distressing conditions." (MJRY, 14–15.)

A marvelous example of one who suffered death rather than to renounce her religion was Mrs. Orson Spencer:

Orson Spencer was a graduate from an eastern college, who having studied for the ministry, became a popular preacher in the Baptist Church. Meeting with a Mormon elder, he became acquainted with the teachings of Joseph Smith and accepted them. Before doing so, however, he and his highly educated young wife counted the cost, laid their hearts on the altar and made the sacrifice! How few realize what it involved to become a Mormon in those early days! Home, friends, occupation, popularity, all that makes life pleasant, were gone. Almost overnight they were strangers to their own kindred.

After leaving Nauvoo, his wife, ever delicate and frail, sank rapidly under the ever accumulating hardships. The sorrowing husband wrote imploringly to the wife's parents, asking them to receive her into their home until the Saints should find an abiding place. The answer came, "Let her renounce her degrading faith and she can come back, but never until she does."

When the letter was read to her, she asked her husband to get his Bible and to turn to the book of Ruth and read the first chapter, sixteenth and seventeenth verses: "Entreat me not to leave thee or to return from following after thee; for whither thou goest I will go, and where thou lodgest I will lodge. Thy people shall be my people and thy God my God."

Not a murmur escaped her lips. The storm was severe and the wagon covers leaked. Friends held milk pans over her bed to keep her dry. In those conditions, in peace and without apparent suffering, the spirit took its flight and her body was consigned to a grave by the wayside. (MJRY, 17–18.)

No accurate earthly record is available of the number of Saints who died from exposure or lack of proper care during this winter encampment or the subsequent trek across the plains to the Rocky Mountains. However, He who knows all things has a complete record of all who suffered and died as a result of their membership in His kingdom on earth.

The gravity of their situation in Nauvoo forced the Saints to sell valuable property at what has been described as less than sheriff's sale prices. These were the "lucky" ones. Many others simply abandoned their homes, lands, and other possessions.

Brigham Young wrote: "Our homes, gardens, orchards, farms, streets, bridges, mills, public halls, magnificent Temple, and other public improvements, we leave as a monument of our patriotism, industry, economy, uprightness of purpose, and integrity of heart; and as a living testimony of the falsehood and the wickedness of those who charged us with disloyalty to the constitution of our country, idleness and dishonesty" (NB, 222).

The refined character of the Saints was exemplified in an incident involving Wilford Woodruff. As furniture was being carried from an upstairs room in the beautiful home he was abandoning, a heavy piece of furniture was dropped. The leg crashed through the floor and damaged the ceiling in the room below. Elder Woodruff had the damage repaired "because," said he, "when men enter my house I want them to know that people of refinement lived here." (NB, 231.)

The year of 1846 found the Saints scattered across the plains of Iowa and Nebraska. Temporary settlements were established in three principal locations where crops were planted in preparation for the final move further west. About 145 miles west of Nauvoo, the settlement of Garden Grove was established. Twenty-seven miles further west, the Saints organized the community of Mt. Pisgah. This site was named by Parley P. Pratt, who, viewing it from a rocky knoll, was reminded of Moses seeing the promised land from atop Pisgah (Deuteronomy 3:27).

A major encampment was established on the west side of the Missouri River with the permission of the Indians and was named Winter Quarters (now known as Florence, Nebraska). The Saints also settled on the eastern side of the Missouri River, opposite Winter Quarters. They named this site Kanesville; it is known today as Council Bluffs, Iowa.

The Fall of Nauvoo

"Nearly twelve thousand Saints had crossed the river by mid-May [1846], and more than six hundred remained in Illinois. Some were detained by illness or poverty and a few sympathized with the seceders, but to some anti-Mormons it appeared the total evacuation might not be accomplished. This precipitated a final confrontation. Guerrilla warfare was revived against isolated settlers. Then, in June, the mobbers gathered four hundred volunteers, marched to Nauvoo, and demanded surrender. The remaining Nauvoo residents quickly united under former Nauvoo Legion officers and prevented an invasion, but the attacks against farmers in outlying areas continued." (SLS, 221.)

The marauders who attacked Nauvoo and her surrounding settlements did not distinguish the Latter-day Saints from the "new citizens" who had purchased property from the departing citizens; both groups were subject to the harassment of these hooligans.

In July mobbers attacked and brutally beat a group of Mormons and non-Mormons who were outside the city limits gathering grain. When the participants of this outrage were arrested, four Mormon men were kidnapped in retaliation and held hostage for fourteen days as a guarantee of safety for the arrested mobocrats. The hostages were beaten, starved, and offered poisoned food during their captivity. The Mormons escaped, but the mob members never came to trial.

A state militia officer described another beating: "A man near sixty years of age, living about seven miles from [Nauvoo], was taken from his house . . . , stripped of his clothing, and his back cut to pieces with a whip, for no other reason than because he was a 'Mormon,' and too old to make successful resistance. Conduct of this kind would disgrace a horde of savages." (ECH, 414.)

An open battle commenced in Nauvoo on 10 September 1846 and continued for several days as a mob tried to take the city by force. During the ensuing skirmishes three citizens of Nauvoo lost their lives: William Anderson; his fifteen-year-old son, August; and David Norris. Captain Anderson had distinguished himself in the battle of Nauvoo. He boldly leaped from behind fortifications and urged the defenders to follow him. Seeing this act of bravery, one man leaped forward and shouted: "Hurrah for Anderson! Who wouldn't follow the brave Anderson!" This rallied others to the defense. (RFN, 364.)

In order to avoid further bloodshed, and seeing the futility of further resistance, the citizens of Nauvoo finally agreed to a mediated truce and surrendered their city on 17 September. Although the treaty only specified the removal of Mormons from the city, the non-Mormon "new citizens" were similarly expelled by the mobbers. "Some of them were ducked in the river, being in one or two instances actually baptized in the name of the leaders of the mob, others were forcibly driven into the ferry boats, to be taken over the river, before the bayonets of armed ruffians." (CHC 3:18.)

One victim of the mob's venomous activities described the terror of the citizens of Nauvoo: "We expected an indiscriminate massacre was commencing. Myself and others who were sick were carried by friends into the tall weeds and into the woods, while all who were able to do so hid themselves. Many crossed the river, leaving everything behind them. As night approached we returned to our shelter. But, O God, what a night to remember!"

The sick man, Thomas Bullock, then described the events of the following day:

> The next morning at nine o'clock saw me, my wife, my four children, my sister-in-law Fanny, my blind mother-in-law, all shaking with the ague in one house, only George Wardell to do anything for us, when a band of about thirty men, armed with guns, with fixed bayonets, pistols in belt, the captain with sword in his hand, and the stars and stripes flying about,

marched opposite my sheltering roof. The captain called and demanded that the owner of the two wagons be brought out. I was raised from my bed, led out of doors, supported by my sister-in-law and the rail fence. I was then asked if those goods were mine. I replied, "They are." The captain then stepped to within four feet of me, pointing his sword at my throat, while four others presented their guns with bayonets within two feet of my body, and said, "If you are not off from here in twenty minutes my orders are to shoot you." I replied, "Shoot away, for you will only send me to heaven a few hours quicker, for you may see I am not for this world many hours longer." The captain then told me, "If you will renounce Mormonism you may stay here and we will protect you." I replied, "This is not my house; yonder is my house," pointing to it, "which I built and paid for with the gold that I earned in England. I never committed the least crime in Illinois, but I am a Mormon, and if I live I shall follow the Twelve [Apostles]." Then said the captain, "I am sorry to see you and your sick family, but if you are not gone when I return in half an hour, my orders are to kill you and every Mormon in the place."

But oh, the awful cursing and swearing these men did pour out! I tremble when I think of it. George and Edwin drove my wagons down to the ferry and were searched five times for firearms. The mob took a pistol, and though they promised to return it when I got across the river, I have not seen it to this day. While on the bank of the river I crawled to the margin to bid a sister who was going down to St. Louis goodbye. While there a mobber shouted out, "Look! Look! there is a skeleton bidding death goodbye." So you can imagine the poor sickly condition of both of us. (NB, 238–39.)

Driven from their homes with virtually no supplies, the destitute Saints gathered on the Iowa side of the Mississippi River and waited for help from the settlements to the west. The Lord in His mercy did not forget them. Just as He had provided food for ancient Israel (Exodus 16:12–13; Numbers 11:31–32), He helped these suffering Latter-day Saints in their need. On 9 October flocks of quail providentially appeared in the camp, providing much-needed food until relief wagons came to aid the suffering Saints.

The Winter of 1846–47

The harsh conditions of the winter of 1846–47 took their toll in suffering and death among the Latter-day Saints living in their temporary settlements in Iowa and Nebraska. Yet even before the cold of winter set in, many had lost their lives to disease and dietary deficiencies.

Winter Quarters was located near the marshy waters of the Missouri River bottoms, or as the Saints called them, the "Misery Bottoms." Malaria was a major problem, along with scurvy, or "Blackleg," as it was called. Potatoes and horseradish helped control the latter condition.

"Winter Quarters was the Valley Forge of Mormondom," said one who was there. "Our home was near the burying ground; and I can remember the small mournful-looking trains that so often passed our door. I also remember how poor and same-like our habitual diet was: corn bread, salt bacon, and a little milk. Mush and bacon became so nauseating that it was like taking medicine to swallow it; and the scurvy was making such inroads amongst us that it looked as if we should all be 'sleeping on the hill' before spring, unless fresh food could be obtained." (MJRY, 41.)

Today, in what is known as the Mormon Pioneer Memorial Cemetery, there are 600 names on the plaque honoring the pioneers who died at Winter Quarters. A statue of a grieving pioneer mother and father huddled over the fresh grave of their infant child gives a grim reminder of the suffering the Saints endured for their faith. A monument at Mt. Pisgah memorializes the graves of some 250 who are counted as martyrs for their faith. Uncounted deaths also occurred at the other settlements established by the exiles from Illinois.

One of the many who died that winter was Newel Knight. He passed away at the settlement of Ponca as a result of contracting pneumonia. Newel's mother, Polly, was the first Church member to die in Missouri in 1831, and his father died at Mt. Pisgah just a few months before Newel's death. Newel had been faithful from the earliest days of the restoration of the Church. During his eventful life he had experienced the power of the priesthood of God and had seen heavenly manifestations, including a vision of the Lord Jesus Christ. On the occasion of seeing the Savior, it was made known to Newel that he would one day enter "into his presence to enjoy His society for ever and ever" (HC 1:85). Newel passed away on 11 January 1847.

Saints at Sea

Shortly after the first missionaries arrived in England in 1837 to begin the task of proclaiming the gospel to the inhabitants of far-flung shores, converts began leaving their homelands and sailing to "Zion." Many left family and friends to make the arduous journey and came at great financial sacrifice. Some never arrived at their "promised land," dying en route and having their bodies committed to the seas to await the day of resurrection.

Many emigrants temporarily settled on the east coast, waiting the day when they had sufficient financing to take them west with the main body of the Church. As the Saints in Nauvoo contemplated their exodus, Elder Orson Pratt was busy in New York helping to organize an expedition that would sail around Cape Horn to the California coast. Samuel Brannan, publisher of the *Prophet,* the Church newspaper in New York, was chosen to head up the undertaking.

On the very day the first wagons left Nauvoo—4 February 1846—the chartered ship *Brooklyn* pulled out of New York harbor with its human cargo of Latter-day Saints, bound for the West. The group consisted of seventy men, sixty-eight women, and one hundred children. The group was kept in quarters below deck. The ceiling was so low that mature adults could not stand upright. Each family had its own little cramped cubicle, and all shared the "big table" where they ate, sang, and prayed on their 24,000-mile, six-month journey.

The journey was fraught with hardships. At night the women and children had to be lashed to their berths to prevent them from being thrown out. Furniture would often roll about precariously as the ship tossed about on stormy seas. On at least one occasion the captain of the vessel despaired for their safety and warned all to be prepared to die. Although there was obvious fear on such occasions, the faith of the Saints calmed troubled souls if not troubled

106

seas. The captain is said to have responded, "They are either fools and fear nothing, or they know more than I do." (KGR, 362.)

Near the end of the journey, living conditions were so bad that the drinking water had to be strained between one's teeth because it was so thick. Clothing and bodies were washed in salt water, and rats, roaches, and vermin were everywhere. As a result of this infestation, "eternal vigilance was the price imposed upon every mouthful" that was eaten (KGR, 363). Sickness was rampant.

There are differing accounts as to the number who died during the long voyage, but the following are the names of some said to have perished: Isaac Aldrich, Silas Aldrich, Elias Ensign, Eliza Ensign, Laura Goodwin, Edwin Narramore, child of Sarah Burr, child of Jerusha Fowler, child of Mr. and Mrs. Joseph Nichols, two children of Mr. and Mrs. John R. Robbins, and a child of Mr. and Mrs. George K. Wimmer (CM, 8–10; ETN, 30, 34).

All of the above persons but Laura Goodwin were buried at sea. Her grave was dug on Robinson Crusoe Island in the Juán Fernández Islands located in the Southern Hemisphere.

It is of interest to note that two babies were born during the voyage. One, born on the east coast waters, was named John Atlantic Burr. The other, born on west coast waters, was named Pacific Georgiana Robbins.

Handcart Pioneers

By 1849, two years after the first Latter-day Saints arrived in the Great Basin, there were still thousands of refugees from Illinois living in temporary camps on the plains. A plea went out for funds to help bring these stranded Saints to the main body of the Church.

The following year the Perpetual Emigration Fund was established. This was a revolving fund from which emigrants could obtain loans that were to be repaid as they in turn assisted others. The fund was particularly helpful to those on foreign shores who desired to gather to the Rocky Mountains.

As early as 1851 the leaders of the Church recognized the need to cut costs and recommended that those too poor to purchase oxen- or horse-drawn wagons consider buying handcarts. These small carts, containing all the earthly possessions of the poor pioneers, were to be pulled and pushed across the plains.

Although there were isolated instances where handcarts had been used, it was not until about 1856 that the movement began in earnest. On 9 June 1856, 266 handcart pioneers departed from Iowa City and began their trek across the plains. They were followed within a matter of days by two succeeding companies. "A few deaths among the aged and infirm occurred on the way, but these companies all arrived in Salt Lake City in good condition and happy to be in Zion" (ECH, 399).

Unfortunately, two other handcart companies left later in the season with tragic consequences. The James G. Willie company left Iowa City on 15 July and from Florence [Winter Quarters] on 19 August. Edward Martin led another company about two weeks later. Both groups had anticipated arriving in the Salt Lake Valley before winter weather was upon them—a fatal miscalculation.

The first frosts of the year were encountered by the middle of September, and the weather was fast turning very cold. As the journey became more difficult, loads were lightened in order to increase the pace of travel. What few possessions the poor emigrants had were left along the trail. In addition, because many of the handcarts had been fashioned from unseasoned wood, many of them broke down and had to be abandoned, which placed additional burdens upon those who had functioning carts.

With little to protect them from the storms, clothing and bedding became frozen and remained that way. Many were found frozen to death after a fitful night's sleep and were buried in shallow, unmarked graves where they became easy prey for wolves and other predators. Wood, especially that which was dry and burnable, was hard to find, and many were the nights when there were no fires to warm the frozen bodies or thaw out stiff clothing.

Food became scarce, and the people were forced to forage for anything that was edible. One pioneer girl reported that her family's meal one evening consisted of broth that had been boiled from the head of a dead cow and flavored with sage brush.

By October the Martin company had reached the "deplorable condition" where they were "seven hundred miles from Salt Lake and [had] only nine days full rations" left (WV, 229). The Willie company was in similarly desperate circumstances. Missionaries who encountered the suffering Saints brought word to the leaders of the Church in Salt Lake City of the precarious situation of the handcart pioneers, and relief parties were immediately organized. Joseph A. Young and Stephen Taylor were sent as advance messengers to alert the stricken emigrants that help was on its way. A relief train soon followed. A severe storm forced the emigrants of the Willie company to seek shelter in hollows and willow thickets near the Sweetwater River.

Not knowing the absolute destitution of the emigrants, and that they were perishing only a few miles distant, the relief train had gone into encampment, awaiting the arrival of the handcart company or the passing of the storm. Meantime Captain Willie with a single companion, started westward in search of the relief train. He found it; whereupon all possible haste was made to reach the sufferers. It was the evening of the third day after his departure that Captain Willie returned at the head of fourteen well loaded wagons. Their arrival came none too soon, if the camp was to be saved from utter destruction: for the ravages of hunger, dysentery, and exhaustion were threatening the extinction of the helpless emigrants. (CHC 4:93.)

Six wagons remained with the Willie company and the other eight went on to relieve the sufferers of the Martin company. There were not sufficient wagons to carry the sick and suffering Saints, and many had to continue to trudge through the snow while pushing their handcarts.

When the Martin company arrived at the Sweetwater on 3 November, a scene of sheer mental torture greeted their eyes. They found the freezing waters filled with chunks of ice. To the already frozen and weakened travelers this seemed like too much to bear. In anguish and despair many simply slumped to the ground and wept."How can we survive such an added hardship?" they wondered.

"Three eighteen-year-old boys belonging to the relief party came to the rescue, and to the astonishment of all who saw, carried nearly every member of that illfated handcart company across the snowbound stream. The strain was so terrible, and the exposure so great, that in later years all the boys died from the effects of it. When President Brigham Young heard of this heroic act, he wept like a child, and later declared publicly, 'That act alone will ensure C. Allen Huntington, George W. Grant and David P. Kimball an everlasting salvation in the Celestial Kingdom of God, worlds without end.' " (IE, 17:288.)

This unselfish act of heroism will forever enshrine their names among the martyrs who have willingly suffered and given their lives to save others.

The first group arrived in Salt Lake City on 9 November and the following group about three weeks later. On their arrival "the bishops of different wards took every person who was not provided with a home to comfortable quarters. Some had their hands and feet badly frozen but everything which could be done to alleviate their suffering was done, and no want was left unadministered to." (CHC 4:94.)

B. H. Roberts reports that "the exact number of those who perished in this company is not of record in our official annals; and it is difficult to fix upon any approximate number with certainty." The best estimate is that 77 of the Willie company perished and 150 of the larger Martin company lost their lives. (CHC 4:101–2.)

This Is the Place

On 23 July, 1847, the first group of pioneers emerged from the mountains east of the present site of Salt Lake City and began their descent into the desolate, uninviting valley that would become their home.

"There was little vegetation save the stubby growth of salt-grass, grease-wood and sage that covered the valley, and the few willows and cottonwood trees that stood on the banks of the canyon streams. . . . The few emigrants who had passed through the Great Basin had made haste to get beyond and into the more inviting parts of the Pacific coast." (ECH, 366.)

One of the best-known mountain men of that time, Jim Bridger, had suggested to Church leaders that it was "imprudent to bring a large population into the Great Basin until it was ascertained that grain could be raised" (MsHBY, 28 June 1847). Perhaps some reflected on this when their initial efforts to plant crops in the sun-baked desert soil resulted in several plows being broken.

Not many looked upon the Great Basin with much favor. In 1843, Senator George H. McDuffie of South Carolina proclaimed on the floor of the Senate that he would not "give a pinch of snuff for the whole territory" (ECH, 367).

Even Brigham Young's own wife, Clara Decker Young, was less than enthusiastic about the prospects of establishing her home in this arid desert. "I have come 1200 miles to reach this valley and walked much of the way," she murmured, "but I am willing to walk a thousand miles farther rather than remain here" (RC, 262).

In spite of the misgivings of some, the vision of prophets was clear. In 1842 Joseph Smith uttered the following prophecy: "The Saints would continue to suffer much affliction and would be driven to the Rocky Mountains, many would apostatize, others would be put to death by our persecutors, or lose their lives in consequence of exposure or disease, and some of them would live to go and assist in making settlements and build cities and see the Saints become a mighty people in the midst of the Rocky Mountains" (ECH, 267–68).

The Old Testament prophet Isaiah had also prophesied concerning the Rocky Mountain refuge of the future followers of the God of Abraham, Isaac, and Jacob. "And it shall come to pass in the last days," said this ancient seer, "that the mountain of the Lord's house shall be established in the top of the mountains, and shall be exalted above the hills; and all nations shall flow unto it" (Isaiah 2:2). This "mountain of the Lord's house" was established in the Salt Lake Valley (DCE, 372).

Brigham Young, prophet of the Lord, the modern-day Moses who led the latter-day children of Israel to this seemingly not-so-promising land, was clear in his vision of what this land could become. He had given specific instructions to the two Apostles who first entered the valley regarding where they should make camp and begin planting even before he himself had set foot on

111

her soil. As he physically viewed the valley for the first time on 24 July, he gazed in silence for a few moments and then with the witness of the Spirit proclaimed, "This is the right place!"

Brigham Young's seeric vision of what the Salt Lake Valley could become was further exemplified just four days after his arrival. Walking across the area that one day would become one of the nation's most visited landmarks—Temple Square—the prophet poked his cane in the ground and declared: "Here will be the Temple of our God!" He then noted that the city could be "laid out perfectly square north and south, east and west" from that spot.

Several years later, President Young related the following to the Saints gathered on the temple site for cornerstone laying ceremonies: "I scarcely ever say much about revelations, or visions, but suffice it to say, five years ago last July [1847] I was here, and saw in the Spirit of the Temple not ten feet from where we have laid the Chief Corner Stone. I have not inquired what kind of a Temple we should build. Why? Because it was represented before me. I have never looked upon that ground, but the vision of it was there. I see it as plainly as if it was in reality before me." (JD 1:132–33.)

As one compares the reservations found in the minds of many regarding this barren land to the faith and vision exhibited by those who knew from a higher Source that they were in the right place, one is reminded of a divine declaration: "For my thoughts are not your thoughts, neither are your ways my ways, saith the Lord. For as the heavens are higher than the earth, so are my ways higher than your ways, and my thoughts than your thoughts." (Isaiah 55:8–9.)

Deaths in the Great Basin

Hardships and tragedies did not cease once the pioneers entered the Great Basin. The death of three-year-old Milton H. Therlkill on 11 August 1847 is thought to be the first loss of life in the Salt Lake Valley. The lad had wandered from camp and was drowned in the waters of a nearby creek.

Those who died at the end of their journey were not the only ones whose remains were placed to rest beneath the desert soil. In October 1847, Jedediah M. Grant arrived in the valley with a crude coffin tied to the side of his wagon. It contained the body of his wife, Caroline, who had died on the plains. Her dying request was that her body should be carried to the Saints' "promised land" for burial. Like the ancient Israelites who carried the body of Joseph to his "promised land" for burial (Genesis 50:24–25; Joshua 24:32), Jedediah fulfilled his wife's wish. Like others who had perished on the plains, "she died a martyr for the truth."

Jedediah Grant also lost a little daughter to death during the difficult journey. He was unable to bring her body into the valley along with that of his wife, and so he returned to the plains to retrieve her remains. "To his great sorrow he discovered that the wolves had dug up her body, devoured it, and scattered her bones so there was nothing left to bring." (LGL, 19.)

Missionary Martyrs

Peaceful coexistence with the natives of the Great Basin was a priority with Church leaders. The Saints had been welcome guests on Indian lands in Iowa and Nebraska and were desirous of being good neighbors with the Indian tribes that occupied the Great Basin. Besides, they felt a strong sense of brotherhood with these people whom they considered to be descendants of the people of the Book of Mormon.

In general conference, April 1855, forty-one men were called to bring the gospel to the roving bands of Ute Indians who lived in what was known as the Elk Mountains (now called the La Sal Mountains). They arrived in Moab in what is now the southeastern part of the state of Utah in the summer of 1855 and set up camp. Friendly relations were established with the Indians and several months went by without incident. However, in September there began to be a noticeable change in the Indian's attitude toward the missionary-settlers.

Open warfare broke out when one of the missionaries, James W. Hunt, was shot in the back and killed by a heretofore friendly

Indian on the outskirts of the settlement. Before they could return to the safety of the camp, two other missionaries, Edward Edwards and William Behunin, were slain. The Indians then burned haystacks and ran off livestock. The following day, the remaining missionaries abandoned Moab and returned to the safety of Manti. (CN, Feb. 16, 1974, p. C-16.)

Two missionaries passed away of natural causes while serving missions among the Indians. Elder Robert C. Petty died on 6 February 1856, and Elder Washington N. Cook passed away on 4 September 1858. On 2 November 1860, Elder George Albert Smith, Jr., was murdered by some Navajo Indians. At the time of his death he was serving a mission to the Moquis Indians in what is now Arizona.

CHAPTER EIGHT

Plural Marriage and Misunderstanding

A New Challenge

The Latter-day Saints encountered numerous hardships as they sought to tame the wilderness to which their "modern Moses" had brought them. In addition to the challenge of their physical surroundings, they often faced the more harsh condition of continued hostility and prejudice on the part of the government and the people of the United States who fed upon falsehoods and misunderstandings about the people known as "Mormons."

One of the most difficult doctrines of the restored gospel for nonmembers to understand or to accept was that of plural marriage. The accepted practice of marriage in western civilization during the nineteenth century, particularly among those claiming to be Christian, was that one man and one woman constitute a marriage relationship. It was unthinkable that one man should have multiple wives.

Even many faithful members of The Church of Jesus Christ of Latter-day Saints initially struggled with the doctrine of plural marriage. Brigham Young, for example, was so disturbed when the doctrine was first taught to him that he said, "It was the first time in my life that I desired the grave" (JD 3:266). The man who was later to publicly announce the practice of plural marriage, Orson Pratt, "came close to abandoning the faith after his first encounter with the new marriage system" (ME, 198).

What changed these men and others from a position of disbe-lief and reluctance to one of faithful support? Perhaps the follow-ing account by Lucy Walker Smith, one of Joseph Smith's plural wives, gives a clue:

> When the Prophet Joseph Smith first mentioned the prin-ciple of plural marriage to me I felt indignant and so expressed myself to him, because my feelings and education were averse to anything of that nature. But he assured me the doctrine had been revealed to him of the Lord, that I was entitled to receive a testimony of its divine origin myself. *He counseled me to pray to the Lord which I did, and thereupon I received from Him a powerful and irresistible testimony of the truthfulness and divinity of plural marriage,* which testimony has abided with me ever since. (ETN, 365; italics added.)

An ancient prophet reminds us that some things are "hard to be understood, save a man should inquire of the Lord" (1 Nephi 15:3). As in all things, when the Spirit ratifies a difficult doctrine, humble hearts accept while the haughty and hardhearted continue to complain that "the Lord maketh no such thing known unto us" (1 Nephi 15:9).

Divine Approbation of Plural Marriage

Divine sources had instructed the Prophet Joseph Smith re-garding plural marriage as early as 1831, but he did not com-mence its practice until 5 April 1841, when he married Louisa Beaman. Evidently this latter-day prophet had wondered why some ancient prophets—such as Abraham, Isaac, and Jacob—had taken more than one wife. Although the Lord gave His seer a rev-elation on the matter (D&C 132), the answer to Joseph's inquiry was essentially already available in the sacred book he had been called to translate just a few years earlier—the Book of Mormon.

Through the ancient prophet Jacob the Lord had instructed His people that it was an abomination for a man to have more than one wife *unless* God commanded him otherwise (Jacob 2:23–30). Such exceptions are essentially divinely decreed when the Lord wants to "raise up seed" to Himself (Jacob 2:30; see also D&C 132:63). Thus, while the general pattern is for a man to have but one wife, there are occasions when Deity may deem it otherwise. The Lord later revealed that the right to grant such exceptions to His Saints could only come through the prophet who held the keys of this power (D&C 132:7). This prophet would be the duly acknowledged President of The Church of Jesus Christ of Latter-day Saints, the seer who holds all keys of priesthood authority available to man.

Many well-meaning historians and social scientists, in addition to some misguided theologians, have attempted to explain the reasons for the practice of plural marriage among the Latter-day Saints. Regardless of how plausible some of their explanations may be, there is really only one basic reason for the practice coming into existence—God commanded it! Yes, even knowing the persecution that its practice would bring upon His Saints, He willed that they live according to its laws. Some day we shall understand all of His reasons, but in the meantime we walk by faith and accept the fact that His ways and His thoughts are higher than are ours (Isaiah 55:8–9).

From Secrecy to Public Acknowledgment

Following his receipt of the revelation on plural marriage in 1831, Joseph Smith had spoken about the principle to a few close associates. "Some members, told by the Prophet that a new marriage system eventually would be introduced, assumed the prerogative of practicing it without authorization. These aberrations led to some apostasy during the mid-1830s." (SLS, 69–70.)

The rumor mill began to spread its malicious message of unorthodox marriages and sexual practices among the Mormons. The Church responded in 1835 with an official statement on marriage that "correctly asserted that the law of the Church *at that time* affirmed only the monogamous marriage relationship" (SLS, 70; italics added).

Following his plural marriage to Louisa Beaman in 1841, the Prophet introduced the doctrine of plural marriage to a few select men and women whose character and faith he trusted. As previously mentioned, the doctrine was not readily accepted. But those who paid the price to receive a testimony of its truthfulness began, with the Prophet's blessing, to practice the principle.

The practice was not publicly acknowledged until eight years after Joseph Smith's life was brought to an untimely close. Then, on 29 August 1852, Elder Orson Pratt delivered a public sermon in which the practice was not only announced but also staunchly defended. Elder Pratt emphasized that plural marriage was not to "gratify the carnal lusts and feelings of man, that there was but one man—the prophet of God—who held the keys of authorizing such marriages, and that the Lord had set "bounds and restrictions" to the practice of plural marriage (ECH, 395).

Numerous estimates have been given regarding the number of Mormon men and women who participated in plural marriages. The debate will probably never end—at least in mortality. However, two respected Mormon historians have said, "Based on the best information now available, we estimate that no more than 5 percent of married Mormon men had more than one wife; and since the great majority of these had only two wives, it seems reasonable to suppose that about 12 percent of Mormon married women were involved in the principle" (ME, 199). Some of these marriages were contracted on the basis of "eternity only," which meant that there was no conjugal living in mortality.

Public Opposition to Plural Marriage

The Church's public announcement that it believed in and was practicing plural marriage created a public outcry from far and near. "From the islands of the sea; from Denmark, Sweden and Norway; from distant India as well as from England and the United States came reports of opposition and of increased persecutions ostensibly justified because of the church's announced belief in the doctrine and practice of plural marriage" (CHC 4:58). Even within the Church there were a number who apostatized because they could not accept the doctrine.

By 1856, public reaction against plural marriage had reached such a peak that the Republican Party took an official stand against polygamy and slavery—"the twin relics of barbarism."

The Assassination of Parley P. Pratt

The first person to die as a result of opposition to plural marriage was Elder Parley P. Pratt of the Quorum of the Twelve Apostles. In the summer of 1854, Elder Pratt arrived in San Francisco to preside over the Pacific Mission of the Church. The local members provided food and other supplies to the Pratt family. Among those rendering assistance was a recent convert, Eleanor McLean.

Eleanor had married Hector McLean in 1841 but separated from him three years later because of his drunkenness. They were later reconciled on promises of Hector's reform. Eleanor accepted the restored gospel in 1851 but was prevented from joining the Church by her husband, who purchased a sword and threatened to use it to kill her and any man who should try to baptize her. Hector's tyrannical tirades against the faith his wife had embraced led him to burn any Church books he found and to beat his wife. He was also known to have locked her out of the house.

For some reason, he relented and allowed her to be baptized on 24 May 1854. However, he stipulated that no Mormon songs be sung in his home and that no Church literature be allowed in the house.

Shortly after he arrived, Elder Pratt assigned one of his missionaries, John R. Young, to help Eleanor. The young Elder was promised that by listening to the promptings of the Spirit he would know what to do. He was also given a blessing by his mission president in which he was promised that "not a hair of his head would be harmed."

Elder Young went forth with the faith of Nephi, not knowing beforehand what he was going to do (1 Nephi 4:6). Upon arriving at the McLean house, he found a sign on the door: Cook Wanted. He applied and was hired to cook, clean, and make the beds. He found a pistol under Hector's bed that the man threatened to use on the first Mormon that set foot in his house. The Elder was fired when his identity as a Mormon missionary was discovered, but no harm came to him. John Young's testimony was helpful to Eleanor at sanity hearings when her husband attempted to have her committed to an asylum, and the money the missionary earned from his employment paid his passage to Honolulu, where he was assigned to serve his mission.

Hector secretly sent the McLean children to live with their grandparents in New Orleans, and Eleanor finally gave up on the failing marriage and left him. She moved to Salt Lake City and later became a plural wife of Parley P. Pratt. In August 1856, she joined Elder Pratt in the Eastern States Mission; with his help, she was able to retrieve her children in New Orleans. She then returned to Utah with the children.

Meanwhile, Hector arrived on the scene and successfully had Eleanor and Parley arrested for "stealing children's clothes." During the trial Hector drew his gun and aimed it at Elder Pratt, but court officers prevented him from firing it. Parley was found innocent of the charges, and, knowing the hatred Hector had for him, the judge urged Elder Pratt to secretly flee. McLean pursued and found him. On 13 May 1857, near Van Buren, Arkansas, he attacked Parley, first stabbing him with a bowie knife and then shooting him as he lay on the ground.

Parley P. Pratt's dying words were an affirmation of his faith: "I die a firm believer in the Gospel of Jesus Christ as revealed through the Prophet Joseph Smith, and I wish you to carry this my dying testimony. I know that the Gospel is true and that Joseph Smith was a prophet of the living God, I am dying a martyr to the faith." (BYUS, 15:248.)

Elder John Taylor, a colleague in the Quorum of the Twelve who had himself once escaped martyrdom, wrote the following tribute to Elder Pratt:

Though we deeply deplore the loss to the Church of such a great and upright man, and the bereavement to his family, yet we mourn not. His life has been one of honor and faithfulness; his days have been well spent in the service of his

God; his name is revered by thousands and tens of thousands, and will be honored by millions yet unborn; while that of his cowardly assasins, and those who have cheered them on to this damning deed, and who now rejoice over the crime, will be loathsome, and a stink in the nostrils of God and good men. (*The Mormon,* May 30, 1957; see also APP, 451.)

Anti-Mormon Legislation

As early as 1860 Congressman Justin Morrill of Vermont introduced antibigamy legislation. The House passed the bill, but the Senate failed to act upon it by the time Congress adjourned the following spring. On 8 April 1862, Congressman Morrill reintroduced his bill, which passed both houses of Congress and was signed into law by President Abraham Lincoln on 1 July 1862.

The bill, aimed specifically at Mormons, made the contracting of a plural marriage punishable by a fine of five hundred dollars and imprisonment for a term of five years. It also forbade religious bodies in United States territories from holding real estate valued in excess of fifty thousand dollars. Although he had signed the legislation, President Lincoln's policy was to let the Mormons alone and the law was not vigorously enforced at first.

There were other efforts to pass legislation aimed at stripping the Latter-day Saints of basic rights. Fortunately, for a season, none of the proposed bills was passed. These bills included the Wade bill, introduced in 1866, which sought to destroy self-government in Utah and prohibit Church leaders from performing marriages. In 1867, the Cragin bill proposed the abolishment of trial by jury for those accused of violating the Morrill bill of 1862. Shortly after this the Ashley bill was introduced, which essentially called for the dismemberment of the Territory of Utah. These bills are but a sampling of the anti-Mormon feeling that was prevalent in the halls of Congress.

One lone voice in Congress, that of James G. Blair of Missouri, sought to support the Saints in their religious beliefs. In 1872 he proposed legislation that would legalize all marriages in Utah and dismiss all charges pending against those who were practicing plural parriage. His bill failed to gain support but was a credit to the man and the state he represented which previously had not been known to be friendly to Latter-day Saints.

On 24 June 1874, President Ulysses S. Grant signed the Poland Law, which essentially took away representation in the judicial system from the people of the Territory of Utah and vested it with the United States marshal, his deputies, and the U.S. district attorney and his assistants. This law was used in the conviction of George Reynolds, private secretary to President Brigham Young.

Prisoners for Conscience' Sake

Elder Reynolds volunteered to be the subject of what was supposed to be a friendly court case to test the constitutionality of the antibigamy act of 1862. Both the Church and the government were anxious to have a court ruling on the issue. George Reynolds was indicted in October 1874. He surrendered to the court and willingly provided evidence against himself of living the law of plural marriage. He was found guilty and ordered to pay a five-hundred-dollar fine and spend one year in prison.

An appeal to the territorial supreme court brought a dismissal, but in October 1875, Elder Reynolds was indicted a second time. This time the judge doubled the sentence—two years in prison—and added the punishment of "hard labor." The case was ultimately appealed to the United States Supreme Court, which handed down a decision on 6 January 1879 affirming the conviction and the constitutionality of the law of 1862. The Court did "remand the case to the supreme court of Utah, with instructions 'to cause the sentence of the district court to be set aside, and a new one entered on the verdict in all respects like that before imposed, except so far as it requires the imprisonment to be at hard labor.' " (ECH, 470.)

In the summer of 1879, George Reynolds was incarcerated for practicing his religious beliefs. He was released in January 1881, being released early because of good behavior. He taught school while in prison and was held in such high esteem that the warden said of him: "Reynolds is worth more than all the guards in keeping order among the prisoners." (ECH, 471.)

Other "prisoners for conscience' sake" had similarly positive effects on the prisons in which they were confined. "At one time there were as many as two hundred 'Mormon' prisoners incarcerated together, which virtually for the time being transformed the Utah Penitentiary from a den of blasphemy and sin into a place of prayer and worship; . . . [the] influence and good example were felt and respected even by the 'toughs,' or real criminals, some of whom would often join in the songs of Zion." (RCH 3:33–34.)

The Edmunds Bill

In March 1882, Congress passed a bill introduced by Senator George F. Edmunds of Vermont. It amended the Morrill bill of 1862, replacing the word *bigamy* with *polygamy*. Polygamous living was described as "unlawful cohabitation," which led to its proponents referring to those who practiced it as "cohabs." Entering into or living in plural marriage was punishable by a fine and imprisonment.

The law was made retroactive so that any man who had ever lived in plural marriage was subject to its consequences. Those who practiced *or* believed in the principal of plural marriage were excluded from jury duty. In addition, the right to vote was denied to such people. It is of interest to note the wording of the test oath for voter applicants: "I do not live or cohabit with more than one woman *in the marriage relation.*" Thus, while a Latter-day Saint might be prevented from exercising his right to vote, an adulterer was exempt from the law's effects.

[Particularly during the 1880s] the government of the United States carried on a campaign of prosecution, that was relentless and even cruel, against all members of the Church who had married plural wives. Men were punished, not for contracting plural marriage since the passage of the law, but for "unlawful cohabitation;" federal officers hunted men and women and dragged them before selected grand juries, where they were shamefully insulted. Even small children did not escape, but were forced to testify and answer improper and indecent questions, with the object in view of obtaining evidence against their parents; and this was done with threats of dire punishment and contempt of court, if they refused. Such actions partook too much of the days of the Spanish inquisition. Paid spies—men of debased character—were employed to gather evidence. Among those who sat on juries to judge the "morals" of the "Mormon" people, were those who were recreant to every law of decency. The petty officers and the judges of the courts carried on a reign of terror in their determination to stamp out the practice of plural marriage, and it appeared that the greatest crime in the world was for a man to acknowledge honestly that he was the husband of more than one wife, and that he diligently and faithfully supported them and their children; while for the libertine and the harlot there was protection by officers of the law. (ECH, 485.)

Homes were invaded in the early hours of the morning by zealots who sought to discover and arrest "cohabs." "Even the bed chambers of modest maidenhood were rudely entered before the occupants could dress, and in some instances the covering of their beds stripped from them in the pretended search for violators of the law" (LJT, 385).

The Edmunds-Tucker Bill

Congress passed a yet more stringent law against the Church that believed in plural marriage and the members who practiced it. On 3 March 1887, the Edmunds-Tucker bill became law. Among its punishing provisions were the following:

- Husbands and wives could be forced to testify against each other.
- "Illegitimate children" (which children born in plural marriages were considered to be) were not entitled to share in their father's estate.

- The property of The Church of Jesus Christ of Latter-day Saints was to be confiscated and disposed of by the secretary of the interior. Places of worship were excluded from this diabolical dictum.
- The Church itself was disincorporated and the Perpetual Emigration Fund was dissolved.
- Women were denied the right to vote.
- "As a condition for voting, holding office or serving on juries, a man was required to pledge obedience to the anti-polygamy laws and to promise not to preach, aid, or advise anything contrary thereto." (ETN, 382–83.)

"The government very graciously permitted the Church to occupy the tithing office and historian's office, at a yearly rental of $2,400; and the Gardo house at $450 a month. The Temple Block was also retained by the payment of a stipulated rent. All this happened in the United States in the year 1887, not in Spain or Holland in the dark ages or the days of the Inquisition." (ECH, 489–90.)

The Underground and Resultant Deaths

To save themselves from the effects of laws they considered unjust, unconstitutional, and in direct violation of their religious beliefs, many of the Latter-day Saints went into hiding. An elaborate underground system was developed whereby those who were being pursued were protected.

Hideouts were prepared in homes, barns, and fields to serve as way stations for the fleeing "cohabs," as they were nicknamed by their pursuers. Secret codes were invented that could be sent between towns to warn of the approaching deputies, and Mormon spotters became proficient at detecting the hunters and spreading the alarm. Not to be outdone, the scores of federal officers brought into the territory to conduct this all-out raid disguised themselves as peddlers or census takers in order to gain entry into homes and hired their own

125

spotters to question children, gossip with neighbors, and even invade the privacy of homes. Ten and twenty-dollar bounties were offered for every Latter-day Saint violator captured. (SLS, 396.)

Among those who were forced to flee and go into hiding was the President of the Church, John Taylor. He preached his last public sermon on 1 February 1885. His feelings were that the Saints should avoid their persecutors just as they would avoid "wolves, or hyenas, or crocodiles, or snakes, or any of these beasts or reptiles." He refused to submit to a law he considered undignified and a direct violation of his religion.

Hounded and harassed, with a bounty placed on his head, President Taylor conducted the affairs of the Church from his various hiding places. Every effort was made by federal officers and their spies to discover the whereabouts of President Taylor. But due to the ever-watchful Church members, their prophet was able to avoid his hunters. "He owed his safety, however, more to the promptings of the Holy Spirit than to the cunning of man. More than once, in obedience to its whisperings, and when to all outward appearances there was no danger to be feared, he would leave his place of temporary abode . . . , [leaving] his enemies mystified as to his whereabouts." (LJT, 390.)

During his exile, President Taylor was deprived of associating with his family, as well as the fellowship of the Church members in general. To those bereft of his companionship, President Taylor wrote: "Some of you have written that you 'would like to have a peep at me.' I heartily reciprocate that feeling, and would like to have a 'peep" at you on this occasion; but in my bodily absence my spirit and peace shall be with you." (LJT, 399.)

President John Taylor, companion of the martyred brothers Joseph and Hyrum Smith, who himself was severely wounded in the assault that took the lives of the Prophet and the Patriarch of the Church, died in exile on 25 July 1887. He was called a "living martyr for the truth" whose death made him "a double martyr." His biographer stated that President Taylor was "killed by the cruelty of officials who have, in this Territory, misrepresented the Government of the United States. There is no room to doubt that if he had been permitted to enjoy the comforts of home, the ministrations of his family, the exercise to which he had been accustomed, but of which he was deprived, he might have lived for many years yet. His blood stains the clothes of the men, who with insensate hate have offered rewards for his arrest and have hounded him to the grave." (LJT, 414.)

One man, Edward M. Dalton, was directly murdered by an "officer of the law" during the troubled days of the 1880s polygamist hunt. His death has been referred to as "the only killing in the polygamy war." (DeS, 321.)

Dalton lived in Parowan, Utah, and was described as "a robust, good-natured citizen [who] did not appear to take seriously an indictment against him for unlawful cohabitation. When he was arrested in early spring of 1886, he announced to the deputy marshal and others who were gathered around him that he was going to escape. He took off his riding boots and with them in his hands outran his pursuers." (AUS, 151.)

He spent the following summer in Arizona and returned to Utah in the winter to care for his family. This was shortly after a man arrested for plural marriage had narrowly escaped being killed by deputy marshal William Thompson.

In the early morning hours of 16 December 1886, Dalton was riding unarmed and bareback through the streets of Parowan, Utah, with a herd of cattle. Suddenly a bullet ripped through the defenseless man's back and he fell dead to the ground, assassinated by Deputy Thompson.

Edward Dalton's tombstone was enscribed as follows:

He Was Shot and Killed, December 16, 1886, in Cold Blood by a United States Deputy Marshal while under Indictment for a Misdemeanor under the Edmunds-Anti-Polygamy Law.
And They Cried with a Loud Voice Saying, O Lord, Holy and True, Dost Thou Not Judge and Avenge Our Blood on Them That Dwell in the Earth. Revelation 6:10 (DeS, 321).

Many Latter-day Saints were arrested and incarcerated during these trying times. However, as previously noted, these prisoners "for conscience' sake" tried to make the best of their circumstances. They held religious services and kept themselves busy teaching and writing. George Q. Cannon completed a book on the life of Joseph Smith, and many budding poets arose. Perhaps the following is not an example of great literary skill by one of the prisoners, but it does represent the feelings of a persecuted yet proud people:

> Though confined in this prison, you are for a while
> Keep cheerful and greet all your friends with a smile,
> The time will soon come when we all will be free
> And the judgments of God on the wicked we'll see.
> We will pity them then and remember how they
> Sought to take both our rights and our families away.
> (AUS, 199.)

Although most of the prisoners were eventually released to return to their homes, some were not quite as fortunate. "Some of the brethren, unused as they were to such close confinement, suffered considerably from sickness during their incarceration; one of them died in his cell, and another immediately after being liberated to return to his home. Others died soon after regaining their liberty, and a great many others contracted diseases with which they died soon after their release. Still others were so broken down physically and mentally, that, although yet alive, they . . . never enjoyed good health [again]." (RCH 3:34.)

The Murder of Elder Joseph Standing

Orson F. Whitney indicated that "one of the earliest results of the agitation that produced [the anti-polygamy legislation] was the murder of a 'Mormon' missionary—Elder Joseph Standing" (PHU, 371).

Elder Standing was serving his second mission to the Southern States, where opposition to the Church was high. Anti-Mormon literature had been circulated "that tended to create the impression among the people that the Church of the Latter-day Saints was outlawed, and her representatives the legitimate objects of mob violence." One southerner opposed to the Church said to Elder Standing, "The government of the United States is against you, . . . and there is no law in Georgia for Mormons." (CHC 5:560.)

One night Joseph Standing had a very foreboding dream about Varnell Station, Georgia. He later described how "clouds of intense blackness gathered overhead and all around [him]." Members of the Church were agitated at his presence and "appeared to be influenced by a sense of great fearfulness." He said he awoke "without . . . being shown the end of the trouble." (LDSBE 3:719.)

On 20 July 1879, twenty-five-year-old Elder Standing and his companion, twenty-two-year-old Rudger Clawson, passed through Varnell Station on their way to a distant conference. They found the members very fearful of the Elders' presence, and none of them would let the missionaries stay overnight.

They spent the night at the home of Henry Holston, a friendly and hospitable nonmember. He informed the Elders that murderous threats had been made against the Saints, and against the Elders in particular. The following morning the Elders were walking along a wooded road when they were accosted by an armed mob of twelve men who forced the missionaries to follow them. As they trudged along, the Elders were threatened with flogging; one of the mobbers without provocation struck Elder Clawson a staggering blow to the back of his head, sending him to his knees.

A young Latter-day Saint girl named Mary Hamlin, who had been sent to warn the Elders of the mob's presence, passed the group on the road, seeing that her message was too late. One of the mobbers threateningly said to her, "You see we have got your brethren. As soon as we dispose of their case we purpose attending to you." With undaunted courage, the brave young girl replied, "The Lord is with them, and my prayers are forever for them." (CHC 5:563.)

> Having reached a clearing, most of the party sat down to rest, while several horsemen rode on to select a suitable place for the proposed whipping. Elder Standing, complaining of thirst, was permitted to drink from a spring near by, and had

129

just returned to his seat upon the ground when the horsemen reappeared. "Follow us," they said. Standing, rendered desperate by the situation, now sprang to his feet, wheeled around, and clapping his hands together, shouted "Surrender!" Quick as a flash, a man at his left arose, thrust a pistol into his face and fired; the ball piercing the brain. He reeled twice and fell. All eyes were then turned upon Clawson. "Shoot that man!" exclaimed the leader. Instantly a dozen guns were leveled at the missionary, who showed amazing intrepidity. Looking calmly into the frowning muzzles, he said, "Shoot." His coolness saved him. The guns were lowered, and the mob gathered in a group to consult, leaving Clawson to wait upon his dying companion. While he went for assistance to the house of a friend—Mr. Henry Holston—the murderers riddled the dead body with bullets [at least 20] and stabbed it with knives; their purpose, it was thought, being to implicate the entire party and insure unanimity of silence. (PHU, 371–72.)

Although they had fled from the state, three of the murderers were eventually arrested. Elder Clawson testified at their trial as an eyewitness of what had taken place. At the conclusion of the trial, the results were telegraphed to Salt Lake City by the mission president: "The old, old story. Verdict, not guilty!" (CHC 5:567.)

The martyred missionary was returned to Salt Lake City, where ten thousand people attended his funeral. His remains were buried in the city cemetery, and the following lines by Orson F. Whitney were etched on a monument marking the spot:

Beneath this stone, by friendship's hand is lain
The martyred form of one, untimely slain,
A Servant of the Lord, whose works revealed
The love of Truth for which his doom was sealed.

Where foes beset—When but a single friend
Stood true, nor shunned his comrade's cruel end—
Deep in the shades of ill-starred Georgia's wood,
Fair freedom's soil was crimsoned with his blood.

Our brother rests beneath his native sod,
His murderers are in the hands of God.
Weep, weep for them, not for him whose silent dust
Here waits the resurrection of the just.
(SS 1:90.)

The Tennessee Massacre

Although persecution of Latter-day Saint missionaries continued during the next few years, no martyr's blood was shed again until 10 August 1884, in Cane Creek, Tennessee.

As previously mentioned, pamphlets and books against the Church, as well as newspaper and magazine articles, received wide circulation. Many of these were calculated to excite public passion, perhaps even to justify acts of violence against Church members. "This misrepresentation of the Church of the Latter-day Saints during this period . . . culminated in what is known in the annals of the times as the 'Tennessee Massacre,' directly traceable to an alleged address by a 'Mormon' bishop by the name of 'West,' in Juab, Juab county, about ninety miles south of Salt Lake City. The *canard* [a false or unfounded story circulated to deceive the public], for so it proved to be, was published in the *Salt Lake Tribune,* of Sunday, March 16th, 1884." (CHC 6:86.)

At that time the *Tribune* was a very anti-Mormon newspaper in Salt Lake City that seemed to follow in the fiendish footsteps of the Nauvoo *Expositor* and the Warsaw *Signal* as a promoter of Mormon hating. The *Tribune* published a purported stenographic report of an address allegedly given by "Bishop West" the previous Sunday, in which the bishop openly called for vengeance on the "knavish" Gentiles, declaring they were "eye-sores in the sight of the Lord" (CHC, 6:86–87). The story was allegedly given to the *Tribune* by "a friend" of the newspaper, Tobias Tobey.

Investigation proved there was no Bishop West in Juab and no such meeting had been held. Furthermore, nobody seemed to know the existence of anyone named Tobias Tobey. On 20 March, the *Tribune* published a recanting editorial in which they

131

admitted to the fabricated nature of the story. However, their "apology" was muted with the following malicious message:

"We regret that we have been made the vehicle of this imposture, *but it is so like what is going on all the time and the ordinary talk and feeling of the majority here, only in more concentrated form, that it might have deceived even a saint"* (*Salt Lake Tribune*, 20 March 1884). The newspaper later declared that they did not consider the publication of the fabricated address as libel, "though it was non-genuine. But the genuine is worse than the spurious, as fact is stranger than fiction." (CHC 6:89.)

The "Bishop West" story was circulated in Tennessee by a Reverend Vandevere "who made it an occasion to attack the Saints in the South, and arouse the populace against them. He had been duly advised of the nature of the falsehood, but that made no difference; he continued to repeat the story. The result of his circulation of the *Tribune's* falsehood, was the enacting of a tragedy, at Cane Creek, Lewis County, Tennessee, of a most shocking character." (ECH, 486.)

During the spring and summer of 1884, Elders John H. Gibbs and William H. Jones had enjoyed considerable success in their missionary labors in Cane Creek. Eighteen converts had entered the waters of baptism between April and July. Elder Gibbs had received a threatening letter shortly after his arrival in the area but ignored it on the basis of the following verse, which he said came to his mind from the whisperings of the Spirit:

> We want no cowards in our band,
> Who will our colors fly:
> We call for valiant hearted men
> Who're not afraid to die.
> (TINL, 114.)

Elder Gibbs said to himself, "This speaks for more baptisms." Sure enough, the next day there were three people baptized into the Church. He declared, "It is a true saying among the Elders, 'Where the wolves are, there are sheep near.' "

On Sunday, 10 August 1884, the two Elders were to join with Elders William S. Berry and Henry Thompson in holding religious services in the home of James Condor, a resident of Cane Creek. Elder Jones left for the meeting a little after his companions, who had gone ahead. As he arrived near the Condor residence, he was seized by more than a dozen masked men who demanded to know the whereabouts of the other missionaries, particularly Elder Gibbs.

Meanwhile, people had begun to gather for the meeting, and some preliminary singing had commenced, including these seemingly prophetic lines:

> My life is sought, where shall I flee?
> Lord, take me home to dwell with thee:
> Where all my sorrows will be o'er,
> And I shall sigh and weep no more.
> (TINL, 64.)

The mob attacked without warning, James Condor was seized at the front gate, but he shouted to his son, Martin, and to James R. Hudson, his stepson, to get their guns and resist the attack. As Martin entered the house he found one of the mobbers taking down the boy's gun from its resting place on deer horns over the back door of the livingroom. The two struggled fiercely over the weapon until the young boy was shot down by others of the mob. The confiscated gun was then turned on Elder Gibbs who, with Bible in hand, was shot dead.

A gun aimed at Elder Thompson was seized by Elder Berry and pushed aside, enabling Thompson to flee out the back door and into the woods to safety. However, in saving his friend's life, Elder Berry sacrificed his own—he received the brunt of two shotgun blasts.

James Hudson came down from the attic where he had retrieved his gun and, after struggling with two of the attackers, shot the man who had murdered Elder Gibbs.

The mobber dropped dead, but his fiendish friends killed young Hudson.

The attacking assassins then began firing their guns indiscriminately into the house, viciously wounding Mrs. Condor in the hip and riddling the bodies of the dead.

133

The single guard left in the adjacent woods with Elder Jones, hearing the firing, mingled with the screaming of the women and children, and thinking that a general massacre was going on, evidently became alarmed and permitted his prisoner to escape, accompanying him through a cross country run to a trail leading into the adjoining county of Hickman.

The coroner's inquest over the bodies of the two elders and the two Condor brothers, determined that they came to their death "by gun shot wounds inflicted by unknown parties." The Condor brothers were interred in the orchard surrounding their home, where they had so valiantly sought to defend their friends, the two slain elders. The latter by the coroner's orders were buried in rough coffins on a knoll overlooking Cane Creek, by the roadside, and a little below the Condor residence. (CHC 6:91–93.)

The bodies of the slain Elders were disinterred and retrieved by Elder B. H. Roberts, who did so at the peril of his own life. He had the bodies shipped to Utah, where they received an appropriate burial.

In spite of the heinous nature of a crime which had claimed four innocent lives and seriously wounded a woman, some hard-hearted people continued to show their enmity towards Latter-day Saints. Consider the lack of Christian compassion in these words sent by Eli H. Murray, the anti-Mormon governor of Utah, to the governor of Tennessee:

Lawlessness in Tennessee and Utah are alike reprehensible, but the murdered Mormon agents in Tennessee were sent from here, as they have been for years, *by the representatives of organized crime,* and I submit that as long as Tennessee representatives in congress are, to say the least, indifferent to the punishment of offenders against the national law in Utah, such cowardly outrages by their constituents as the killing of *emigration agents* sent there from here will continue (CHC 6:99).

Contrast the foregoing attitude of vicious vindictiveness with that of leaders of the Church who spoke at the funeral of one of the slain Elders. President George Q. Cannon noted that his heart did not swell with pity for the martyred missionaries, but for their murderers. Knowing "the penalty they have brought upon themselves" through their dastardly deed, President Cannon said, "For them my pity is deep, is profound, is inexpressible."

Speaking of Elders Gibb and Berry, he said: "They have received, or rather will receive crowns of glory, immortal glory. They will be the companions of the Gods. They will sit down with Jesus, the Mediator of the new covenant. By their deaths they will secure an entrance into the society of the Prophets and the Apostles, and the martyrs, the noblest, the holiest, the best, the most exalted of our race. There is no glory that God can give to man, there is no exaltation which God can bestow upon man that these our martyred brethren will not receive." (JD 25:279.)

The two Condor brothers had not yet entered into the waters of baptism prior to their deaths. There seems little doubt that, pending their full acceptance of the gospel of Jesus Christ with its accompanying covenants and ordinances, Martin Condor and John Reilly Hudson will someday share the same kinds of rewards promised to the two missionaries. President Cannon said of them, "I feel that their names should be had in honorable remembrance in Zion, as well as the name of their mother and of their family, for their kindness and their bravery, in the cause of truth, and their names should not perish nor be forgotten" (JD 25:287–88).

More Southern States Martyrs

The next missionary to die in martyrdom was Elder Alma P. Richards. He was a twenty-nine-year-old married man who entered the mission field in October 1887 at great sacrifice. Just days before his departure to the mission field, Alma's youngest son, Alva, passed away. He left his grieving wife, Anna, at home with two other young children.

"Elder Richards was possessed of a social disposition and readily made many friends wherever he went; confiding, frank and gentle he won the hearts of all he came in contact with and was especially a favorite among the saints. . . . His letters to his wife and parents were full of encouragement and good advise, and bore evidence of the spirit that actuated him in his labors." (LDSBE 3:701.)

During the summer of 1888, Elder Richards's traveling companion was released from his mission, and Alma was temporarily left to work on his own. He was last seen alive in the Ragsdale Hotel in Meridian, Mississippi, where he left a package that he said he would pick up two weeks later.

For eleven months his disappearance remained a mystery. Then it was learned that about the time he had turned up missing, a dead body was found near the railroad tracks about eight miles east of Meridian. Inasmuch as no one was able to identify the body, it was buried as a vagrant. Upon later inquiry, the coroner was able to identify a photograph of Alma Richards as the man they had buried the previous summer. The grave was opened and the body was positively identified as that of Elder Richards. His remains were returned home for burial in Milton, Utah.

From the mangled condition of the body, it was supposed that he had been thrown upon the railroad tracks. Whether he was murdered to be robbed or for religious reasons, we do not know. However, inasmuch as he was in the ministry of the Master at the time of his death, he remains a martyr.

The last known man to lose his life by violent means before the turn of the century was George P. Canova. He served as the branch president in Sanderson, Florida. He was described as "one of the most well-to-do men in Baker County, [Florida]." (TINL, 91–92.)

He was mysteriously assassinated one night as he sat in his buggy outside the gate leading to a rented building where a Church conference was to be held. The gun was fired at such close range that the impact literally blew off part of the man's head. No motive was ever discovered for this brutal attack, and no murderer was ever found.

There would yet be threats directed at, and beatings of, Latter-day Saints in the southern states and elsewhere before the turn of the century. For example, Elders William M. Hansen and Harvey C. Carlisle were abducted by an armed mob of men in Harrent County, North Carolina, one November night in 1897. The Elders were marched down the road to a spot where "two ominous-looking long boxes were at the side of the road." Ropes were thrown over the limbs of nearby trees and around the Elders' necks. Then the mobbers went to the other side of the road and began to confer on their diabolical plans.

"Although the night was very still, and no breeze blowing, the two lanterns above the elders suddenly went out. They quickly removed the ropes and crawled into the underbrush and hid." Unable to find the missionaries, the mobbers finally left and the Elders found safety. (CN, March 26, 1977, C-16.)

In spite of the deaths that did occur, perhaps one of the greatest miracles of the nineteenth century is that not more missionaries and members were slain as martyrs to the cause they espoused. Many were saved by responding to the whisperings of the Spirit, and others, such as the two Elders in the story just related, were obviously saved by divine intervention.

Some, with scars on their bodies or tears in their clothing, lived to continue their ministry. Elder John Alexander was beaten and shot at point-blank range near Adairsville, Georgia, but survived. Elder Alexander, under threat of death, refused to deny his testimony. He was granted his request for a final prayer, in which he said, "Oh, my God, if it is thy will that these men should take my life, I am willing to die." As he faced his would-be assassins and closed his eyes, three shots rang out and he fell to the ground.

He survived the attack, discovering that one bullet went through the front of his hat, one went through his open coat, grazing his watch chain, and evidence of the third bullet could not be found. (JI 18:207.)

The Manifesto

In 1841 the Lord revealed the following: "Verily, verily, I say unto you, that when I give a commandment to any of the sons of men to do a work unto my name, and those sons of men go with all their might and with all they have to perform that work, and cease not their diligence, and their enemies come upon them and hinder them from performing that work, behold, it behooveth me to re-

137

quire that work no more at the hands of those sons of men, but to accept of their offerings" (D&C 124:49). Perhaps reflecting on the above scripture, and responding to the promptings of the Spirit, President Wilford Woodruff sought the will of the Lord on the continuing practice of plural marriages.

The answer came! President Woodruff later explained:

> The question is this: Which is the wisest course for the Latter-day Saints to pursue—to continue to attempt to practice plural marriage, with the laws of the nation against it and the opposition of sixty millions of people, and at the cost of the confiscation and loss of all the Temples, and the stopping of all the ordinances therein, both for the living and the dead, and the imprisonment of the First Presidency and Twelve and the heads of families in the Church, and the confiscation of personal property of the people (all of which of themselves would stop the practice); or, after doing and suffering what we have through our adherence to this principle to cease the practice and submit to the law, and through doing so leave the Prophets, Apostles and fathers at home, so that they can instruct the people and attend to their duties of the Church, and also leave the Temples in the hands of the Saints, so that they can attend to the ordinances of the Gospel, both for the living and the dead?

President Woodruff went on to say that the Lord had shown him "by vision and revelation" what would happen to the Church if it continued the practice of plural marriage. He was told in unmistakable terms that now was the time to cease its advocacy. Thus, the official declaration known as the Manifesto was issued in 1890, declaring an end to the practice. "The God of heaven commanded me to do what I did do," declared His prophet. (See "Excerpts from Three Addresses by President Wilford Woodruff Regarding the Manifesto," pp. 292–93, Doctrine and Covenants, 1981 edition.)

While the transition would not be smooth, the door was now ajar to once again begin moving the kingdom forward. To this day there are those who still reject the Church because it once practiced plural marriage. Since those troubled times there have also been some who have not understood the matter of priesthood keys being vested in the Lord's prophet. The members accepted the practice of plural marriage on faith, and they accept its discontinuance on the same principle, knowing that the Lord reveals His will through His authorized, recognized, and duly sustained prophet.

Missionary Martyrs

During the seventy years from the time the Church was organized in 1830 until 1900, a number of missionaries in the mission field lost their lives of natural causes or because of accidents. Each faithful one wears the crown of a martyr.

The vast majority of the martyr missionaries died in the United States. However, missionaries also passed away while serving in the following countries: England, Scotland, Australia, Wales, Denmark, New Zealand, Mexico, Syria, Samoa, Palestine, Germany, Sweden, Switzerland, and the Netherlands.

Elder Loren C. Dunn provides us with some examples from the Samoan Mission that typify the commitment of these missionaries and the sacrifices they were willing to make for the gospel of Jesus Christ (En, May 1975, pp. 25–27).

Katie Eliza Hale Merrill and her husband had only been on their mission for three months when she became severely sick and gave birth to a premature son. Both the child and the mother died the next day, leaving the bereaved husband to finish his mission alone.

Thomas H. and Sarah M. Hilton lost three children while serving a mission to Samoa between 1891 and 1894. While exaltation of these children was assured because they had not yet arrived at the age of accountability (D&C 137:10), it is well to think of the sacrifice their parents were willing to make in behalf of the gospel.

Twenty-nine-year-old Ransom Stevens was serving as president of the Samoan Mission when he fell fatally ill with typhoid fever. He passed away on 23 April, 1894, and one month later his widow, Annie D. Stevens, sailed for America. Five hours after her arrival in Fairview, Utah, she gave birth to a son, having "gone through the whole ordeal in the advanced stages of pregnancy."

William A. Moody and "his bride" Adelia were called from Arizona to serve a mission in Samoa in 1894. A daughter was born to the missionary couple on 3 May 1895, but three weeks later the mother passed away. For the first year of her life, the infant was cared for by local Saints as the father struggled to continue his mission. Then she was placed in the care of some passengers on board a steamer to America where she "will be delivered to loving relatives in Zion."

The sacrifices made by the Saints in the 1800s left a legacy of faith and commitment to the cause of Christ that laid a firm foundation upon which those who followed could stand steady. While they would still face opposition and persecution, and there would yet be more martyrs among them, the members of The Church of Jesus Christ of Latter-day Saints were prepared to meet the new century with full faith in the mission in which they were engaged —bringing the gospel of Jesus Christ to all mankind.

CHAPTER NINE

Twentieth-Century Martyrs

Continuing Hostility

The Manifesto issued by President Wilford Woodruff in 1890, which announced the withdrawal of official Church sanction for contracting further plural marriages, lessened but did not end hostility toward the Church. In 1898 Elder B. H. Roberts, a Latter-day Saint General Authority, was elected to represent the state of Utah in the United States Congress, but his election was challenged by a ministerial alliance in Utah. The group claimed that Roberts's election was a breach of faith with the public because he had three wives.

Roberts's supporters argued that he had married all of his wives prior to the issuance of the 1890 Manifesto, and they reminded his detractors that all political and civil rights had been restored to members of the Church in 1894 by a proclamation of the President of the United States. Nevertheless, a great groundswell of opposition flooded the country, and over seven million signatures were gathered on petitions aimed at denying Elder Roberts his rightful seat in the United States House of Representatives.

On 25 January 1900, Representative-elect Roberts was excluded from the House by a vote of nearly five to one. "A number of those who voted for the majority report confessed that they voted against their consciences and in favor of public clamor that their own political lives might be saved" (ECH, 504).

It is of interest to note that on the same day that Elder Roberts was rejected by prejudiced politicians, Adolph Keilholz, a Latter-day Saint missionary serving in the Netherlands, passed away. He would be the first of scores of martyr missionaries during the 1900s who would commence their labors in mortal mission fields but who would then be called to complete their service beyond the veil.

The first missionary in the 1900s to lose his life at the hands of an assassin was Elder John Dempsey. He was killed by a Campbellite preacher in Eugene, West Virginia, in 1900. His death was reported in the *Deseret Evening News* on 25 September 1900.

Three years after Congress denied Elder Roberts his seat, the legislature in Utah elected Elder Reed Smoot, who was a member of the Council of the Twelve Apostles, to represent Utah in the United States Senate. Once again the public clamored for excluding a Latter-day Saint from his rightful seat in Congress.

Although Elder Smoot had never practiced plural marriage, he was condemned because he was an Apostle in the Church that had preached its practice. Speaking in defense of Elder Smoot, Senator Boies Penrose, a leader in the Senate, said: "I don't see why we can't get along just as well with a polygamist who doesn't polyg as we do with a lot of monogamists who don't monog" (CTC, 31).

Senator Smoot took his Senate seat, but his case was referred to the Committee on Privileges and Elections, where hearings dragged on for several years. The committee voted for Senator Smoot's ouster, but following prolonged debate on the Senate floor, which concluded on 10 February 1907, the senator from Utah received sufficient support to maintain his seat.

Much misunderstanding resulted from the media's unfavorable treatment of the Smoot hearings. Opposition to the Church even spread beyond the shores of America. In 1906 the German government ordered the missionaries out of its country. In 1910 a visiting member of the Quorum of the Twelve Apostles, Elder Rudger Clawson, was imprisoned and then banished from Germany.

In England, Latter-day Saint chapels were vandalized and a branch president was tarred and feathered. Anti-Mormon themes even appeared in literature. A typical plot found in the popular

142

novels of one author "followed the trials of the naive British heroine who at the last moment would be rescued from the deceit of a crafty American missionary" (SLS, 473).

American missionaries continued to suffer persecution during this difficult period. Elder Christen I. Jensen was attacked and thrown into the Arkansas River on 24 January 1910, where he drowned.

Martyrs in Mexico

In 1884 President John Taylor instructed the president of the St. Joseph Stake in Arizona to establish a colony of Saints in Mexico. This was an effort to establish a haven of peace for plural marriage families, free from the severe persecution in the United States at that time. President Taylor explained that it was "better for parts of families to remove and go where they can live in peace than to be hauled to jail and either incarcerated in the territory with thieves and murderers and other vile characters, or sent to the American Siberia [prison] in Detroit to serve out a long term of imprisonment" (MCIM, 52).

There were some initial difficulties with the acting governor of Chihuahua, who, prejudiced by anti-Mormon propaganda and concerned about Americans settling on Mexican land, ordered the Saints expelled. The order was revoked by President Porfirio Díaz in Mexico City following a visit by two members of the Council of the Twelve Apostles.

By March 1886 the colonists had been successful in purchasing property and had named their new settlement Colonia Juárez. An error in the legal documents describing their purchase forced the Saints to move from a more fertile area to one that was rocky, had poor soil, and offered little water. However, just as Moses had provided water for ancient Israel by striking the rocks with his rod (Exodus 17:5–6), the Creator Himself struck the rocks and ground of the area where the colonists were located with an earthquake that opened up fissures and increased the flow of water in the river by one-third. "The Lord was in the earthquake," declared the grateful colonists.

Mexico became a thriving sanctuary for those Saints seeking refuge from persecution north of the border. In addition to Colonia Juárez, the Latter-day Saints established two other colonies: Colonia Dublan and Colonia Díaz.

While the colonists prospered in their new home, life was full of challenges. Peter Nielson, who passed away on 23 January 1886, was the first of many who would die of disease, sickness, or natural causes on Mexican soil. However, there would also be those who died unnatural deaths at the hands of assassins. Early in 1894, young Wesley Norton of Colonia Díaz was murdered and robbed. "This was the first of a series of assassinations suffered by the Latter-day Saints, extending over a series of years" (MCIM, 83–84).

A revolution broke out against the Mexican dictator Porfirio Díaz in 1910, bringing civil and political unrest to the country for the next few years. Although they were counseled to avoid taking sides in the dispute, the American colonists frequently found themselves the victims of this turmoil. "As civil control became disorganized, thievery, robbery, and burglarism flared into open contempt of law or of those attempting to enforce it." (CJ, 165.)

The situation became so intolerable that by 1912 the colonists were forced to forsake their lands and flee north across the border into the United States. The native-born Mexican Latter-day Saints were left to look after the affairs of the Church on their own. One of these was a branch president named Rafael Monroy.

President Monroy and his cousin Vincente Morales were arrested by revolutionists and accused of being members of a rival revolutionary group as well as being Mormons. The two men were given a choice. If they would denounce their religion their lives would be spared. If not, they would die.

For these faithful men, imbued with a testimony of the truthfulness of the work they had embraced, there was but one choice. Their reply: "We cannot deny Jesus Christ nor the testimony we have of the truth."

They were granted a last request to pray, and President Monroy, as depicted in the film *And Should We Die,* uttered these humble words: "Our Father in heaven, we approach thee in the final moments of our lives. Bless us with strength, and forgive these men who are about to take our lives. Bless our families with health and strength that they may live good lives." (SOY [1973], 153; see also ASWD and CTC, 53–54.)

Their prayer for strength to endure this ordeal was answered, and they peacefully faced the raised rifles of their executioners, sacrificing their lives rather than their testimonies or their integrity.

Casualties of World Conflict

Within just a few short years of the end of the Mexican Revolution, much of the entire world was embroiled in armed conflict. In 1914 Austria-Hungary and Germany declared war on Serbia, Russia, and France. Other countries soon became involved in the conflict. Although the United States tried to remain neutral, they were ultimately drawn into what is known as World War I.

Members of The Church of Jesus Christ of Latter-day Saints were called into service on both sides of the conflict. The President of the Church, Joseph F. Smith, counseled those who were called into the armed forces to serve as "ministers of life and not of death; . . . in the spirit of defending the liberties of mankind rather than for the purpose of destroying the enemy" (CR, April 1917, p. 3). It is estimated that between six and seven hundred Latter-day Saints from America lost their lives in this fight for freedom (ECH, 517).

Among those who gave their lives in the conflict was Elder Joseph L. Anderson. He had been set apart to serve in the Eastern States Mission in 1917 but was drafted into the armed forces. He died on the battlefield in Europe on 6 October 1918. He was officially released from his mission after his death.

In Europe, the mission magazine of the Swiss-German Mission was sent to German members serving in the armed forces of their country, keeping them informed of Church news. Its distribution was halted by the German government in 1916. Elder William

145

Kessler was the first former missionary to be slain on the battle-field. He had been called to the Swiss-German mission in 1912 and was inducted into the service of his homeland, where he died on 1 July 1916.

President Smith declared that the German Saints should not be held in contempt for serving in their country's armed forces. "Their leaders are to blame [for the war]," he said, "not the people. The people that embrace the gospel are innocent of these things, and they ought to be respected by Latter-day Saints every-where." (CR, April 1917, p. 11.) There were about seventy-five Latter-day Saints who died in service to the German government during the conflict (CTC, 62).

While an armistice was finally achieved in November 1918, ending this first worldwide conflict, "the devil, who is the father of contention" (3 Nephi 11:29), would once again stir men up to contention just a few years later.

The National Socialists (Nazis) were successful in gaining con-trol of German politics in 1933, and their radical leader, Adolph Hitler, soon had the country embroiled in war. In 1938 he annexed Austria and part of Czechoslovakia, and the following year his ar-mies invaded Poland. Soon all of Europe was involved in warfare.

As the Nazis rose to power, the Latter-day Saints found their worship services increasingly disrupted. Government Gestapo agents monitored Church meetings, and Church leaders were in-terrogated regarding Mormon doctrine. Because of the Nazis' radical anti-Semitic policies, Latter-day Saint teachings regarding "Israel" and "Zion" were suspect. Police ripped pages out of Church hymnbooks that made reference to these terms. Book burning also took place as copies of Elder James E. Talmage's doctrinal book, The Articles of Faith, were confiscated by the government and destroyed.

Missionaries were evacuated from Europe just prior to the out-break of full-scale hostilities. Elder Joseph Fielding Smith of the Council of the Twelve Apostles was in Europe when he received word from the First Presidency to direct the immediate with-drawal of all nonnative missionaries. Amidst the turmoil then pre-vailing throughout Europe, it was nothing short of a miracle that the missionaries were successfully evacuated.

The wife and children of President Wallace F. Toronto of the Czechoslovakian Mission fled to Denmark, where some of the European missionaries were gathering, but he remained behind to assist some missionaries who had been arrested by the Gestapo. Sister Toronto expressed to Elder Smith her concerns about the safety of her husband. Acting in his seeric role as one of the Lord's special witnesses, the Apostle put his arm around the worried wife and said: "Sister Toronto, this war will not start until Brother Toronto and his missionaries arrive in this land of Denmark."

President Toronto and his missionaries boarded the last train to leave Czechoslovakia before the borders were closed and also were on board the last ferry to leave Germany for Denmark. "This was the very day that the Germans commenced their invasion of Poland, the event generally regarded as the beginning of World War II. Thus Elder Joseph Fielding Smith's prophetic promise to Sister Toronto was fulfilled." (CTC, 180–81.)

While Elder Smith could smile with satisfaction over the successful evacuation of the missionaries from Europe, he would soon be saddened over the loss of his own son Lewis, who became one of the many casualties of the conflict. Many mothers and fathers, sweethearts and friends, would send their loved ones off to fight the battle for freedom, never again to embrace them in mortality. It is estimated that over one hundred thousand Latterday Saint men and women served in some phase of the armed forces during the war, and 5,714 were killed, wounded, or reported missing in action (SLS, 545; CTC, 192).

The deaths of these men and women would have an impact on the Lord's work on the other side of the veil. Elder Harold B. Lee, of the Council of the Twelve Apostles, said the following during the dark days of the war:

"It is my conviction that the present devastating scourge of war in which hundreds of thousands are being slain, many of whom are no more responsible for the causes of the war than are our own boys, is making necessary an increase of missionary activity in the spirit world and that many of our boys who bear the Holy Priesthood and are worthy to do so will be called to that missionary service after they have departed this life" (CR, Oct. 1942,

147

p. 73). Such a statement was consistent with the revelation on redemptive work beyond the veil received by President Joseph F. Smith in 1918 (D&C 138:57).

While war waged in Europe, the Japanese began to foment trouble on the other side of the globe. Japan began to aggressively expand its national borders into what was then known as French Indochina. In 1940, Japan signed a ten-year mutual assistance treaty with Germany and Italy, making these three axis nations allies in their aggressions against other countries.

On 7 December 1941, Japanese planes attacked the American naval base at Pearl Harbor in the Hawaiian Islands. This brought the United States into the worldwide conflict on both sides of the globe.

As had been the case during the conflict of World War I, Latter-day Saints once again found themselves thrust into a war that placed faithful members of the Church on both sides of the conflict. As subjects of the sovereign governments where they resided, members of the Church obediently took up arms to fight for their respective fatherlands (Articles of Faith 1:13).

The First Presidency of the Church addressed the issue during general conference in 1942: "On each side they believe they are fighting for home, and country, and freedom. On each side, our brethren pray to the same God, in the same name, for victory. Both sides cannot be wholly right; perhaps neither is without wrong. God will work out in His own due time and in His own sovereign way the justice and right of the conflict, but He will not hold the innocent instrumentalities of the war, our brethren in arms, responsible for the conflict." (MFP 6:159.)

While in historical retrospect it may be easy for those living many years and miles removed from World War II to see the rightness and wrongness of the conflict, it was not that simple for those who were there. In Germany, for example, there were divisive feelings among members of the Church. Unaware of the genocide taking place in Jewish death camps, and being duped by government propaganda, there were those who saw no fault in the German government's policies. On the other hand, some Germans saw their country as the aggressor.

Three such dissenters were young members of the Church living in Hamburg: fifteen-year-old Helmut Huebner, sixteen-year-old Rudolf Wobbe, and seventeen-year-old Karl Schnibbe. The three young men had seen beyond the government propaganda as they listened, by means of a short-wave radio, to broadcasts from England. They began printing and distributing literature telling the German people the other side of the story. Their identity was soon discovered, and they were arrested and charged with high treason on 25 January 1942.

During the trial in Berlin "it was determined that Huebner, who had been a Mormon from birth, was 'highly intelligent and his writings could well have been written by a thirty-year-old professor.' The court thus reasoned that [the youths] should be tried and sentenced as adults." Wobbe was sentenced to ten years in prison but young Huebner, a deacon in the Church, was sentenced to death and was beheaded by the Gestapo on 27 October 1942. (MG, 102–4.)

The actions of the young men brought difficulties to the branch of the Church in Hamburg, and worried local officials excommunicated the boy shortly after his death. The action was reversed by the First Presidency in 1948. Only God will be able to judge the intent of the young man's heart. In the eyes of many, he was a martyr for truth.

The horror and bloodshed of World War II came to a close in two stages. On 8 May 1945, the war in Europe finally ended; three months later, on 14 August, the Japanese surrendered, thus ending the conflict in the Pacific. There would yet be Latter-day Saints who would die in future armed conflicts between nations, but for the moment the sacredness of life would be preserved from such horror.

More Missionary Martyrs

During the first two decades of the twentieth century (1900–1919), approximately 130 missionaries died while serving in the mission field. Most of these deaths were caused by diseases and illnesses such as typhoid fever, pneumonia, and influenza. Perhaps because of improved health standards, there were relatively few deaths of missionaries during the next sixty years (1920–1979). In fact, the total of such deaths during these six decades was less than the total for the first two decades of the 1900s. With the dramatic increase in the number of missionaries serving during the 1980s, the number who died in the mission field also increased. These deaths were chiefly due to accidents, sickness, or other natural causes.

Latter-day Saint missionaries had been relatively safe from assassins until the latter part of the century. A bloody ending came to this period of peace on 13 January 1974 in West Chester, Pennsylvania. Four missionaries were driving to an appointment when a car pulled up behind them and deliberately began crashing into their bumper. The assailant finally succeeded in forcing the missionaries' car into an oncoming lane of traffic, where a fatal accident occurred.

Martyred as deliberately as if a loaded gun had been placed at their heads and the trigger pulled were Elders Leonard Martin, David Grow, and Jeff Buehner. One missionary, Elder Robert Greenwood, survived the crash. The eighteen-year-old driver of the other car was charged with criminal homicide. (SLT, 14 Jan. 1974, B 17.)

One of the most brutal slayings of missionaries occurred later in 1974. Elders Gary Darley and Mark Fischer were serving in Austin, Texas. On 28 October they left their apartment for a dinner appointment and never returned. Their landlady reported the Elders missing on 2 November, and an investigation of their disappearance commenced.

Robert Kleason, the man with whom the Elders were to have had dinner, claimed they never showed up. On 4 November their automobile was found abandoned and stripped. "Thousands of church members searched 30,000 miles of roadway for clues to the elders' whereabouts" (CN, 16 Nov. 1974, p. 3).

Police searched Kleason's home and discovered Elder Darley's name tag with a bullet hole in it as well as blood-stained watches belonging to the two Elders. Other evidence was located, including tires from the Elders' car, a set of scriptures owned by one of

150

the missionaries, and hair samples. A scientific process known as neutron activation analysis proved that the hair samples were from the missing Elders (DN, 29 May 1975, 4 B).

Kleason was arrested and charged with murder. It appears that the two Elders were the victims of his hateful feelings toward the Church. He had been baptized in the fall of 1973 and shortly thereafter spent seven months in three rural jails. According to the district attorney who tried the case, "Kleason killed for revenge on The Church of Jesus Christ of Latter-day Saints because church members did not visit him as often as he thought they should when he spent several months in jail. . . .

"He said Kleason wanted to degrade the church, 'and to show them they couldn't treat him like that. He killed their two missionaries and disposed of their bodies, thinking he couldn't be tried for murder' if the bodies weren't found. . . .

"But Kleason couldn't resist keeping the victims' watches, the prosecutor said. He pictured Kleason as 'a trophy hunter.' " (DN, 3 June 1975, B 11.)

Kleason was found guilty of the murders and sentenced to death. In a travesty of justice, his murder conviction was later overturned on the grounds that a faulty search warrant was used to inspect his trailer. He was later released and, for the time being, walks a free man in our society. (LDSAZ, May 14, 1988, p. 3.) While man's legal system may be flawed, God's eternal justice will ultimately prevail: "For judgment is mine, saith the Lord, and vengeance is mine also, and I will repay" (Mormon 8:20).

Tragedy was avoided in April 1976 when a gunman fired bullets into a Church meetinghouse on the Fort Hall Indian Reservation in Idaho. "Four persons inside the meetinghouse escaped injury, although Bishop John Whitaker said one bullet passed between two men who were three feet apart. He said seven or eight bullets hit the meetinghouse and another struck a parked car." (SLT, 1 April 1976, B 10.)

Later that year, Elder James E. Christensen was severely scalded with hot water and beaten to death in Harrisburg, Illinois (DN, 4 Jan. 1977, A 7).

Another brutal double slaying took place in December 1979 in North Charleston, South Carolina. Sixty-six-year-old Sister Elizabeth W. King and sixty-five-year-old Sister Jane Ruth Cannell Teuscher were physically assaulted and killed by a vile assailant. Both women were widows who wanted to do something "useful" with their lives and had volunteered for missionary service. (CN, 22 Dec. 1979, C 12.)

Elder Vaughn J. Featherstone was asked to speak at the funeral of one of the martyred sister missionaries. He said that dealing with the question of martyrdom was easier than addressing the issue of the violation of her body by a filthy man. As he pondered and prayed about the matter, the Spirit spoke to his soul: "No evil man can pollute a pure soul! A man like that only breaks himself for eternity while she becomes more pure." (From a talk given in the Salt Lake Butler 23rd Ward, 13 January 1980.)

In the deaths of these two faithful sisters, we are reminded of the Latin phrase *Vivit post funera virtus* (Virtue lives after the funeral).

The next violent death of a missionary was that of Elder Boyd J. Batemen in March 1980. Initially there was some question about whether the Elder had actually been assaulted or died of hydrocephalus, but it was determined he had been beaten to death by an assailant.

Murderers took the lives of two Elders during the first six months of 1981. In January Elder Alzira Marques was robbed and shot by three assailants in Brazil. Then in June, seventy-seven-year-old Elder Henry Eliason was knifed in the back in El Cajon, California.

A missionary martyr who was not murdered but who deserves mention is Elder Michael B. Thomas. Elder Thomas, a twenty-eight-year-old Navajo, drowned in 1982 while attempting to save the life of an eleven-year-old girl. Hearing her screams for help, Elder Thomas dove into Big Spring, a pond located about fifteen miles from Roosevelt, Utah. The girl was saved through the assistance of others, but Elder Thomas did not survive.

Fraud, Forgery, and Murder

One of the most infamous chapters in the history of true religion is the story of fraud, forgery, and murder fashioned by one who forsook the way of light to follow the perditious path of darkness.

Early on the morning of 15 October 1985, a respected and much-loved Latter-day Saint bishop and businessman, Steven F. Christensen, arrived at his place of employment in downtown Salt Lake City to find a package outside his door. Noting it was addressed to him, he picked it up. A deafening blast shattered the silence of the hallway where he stood, and shrapnel tore at his flesh as the bomb in the booby-trapped package exploded. The thirty-one-year-old martyr died almost instantly.

It is ironic that Bishop Christensen, known for his magnanimous nature and Christlike character, should fall victim to one who was discovered to be a cold, calculating, criminal whose evil and cunning nature would bring pain, suffering, and sorrow to so many. The death of this caring and committed disciple of Christ at the murderous hands of a modern-day anti-Christ was truly a tragedy.

The death of Bishop Christensen did not end the assassin's murderous deeds. About three hours after the downtown explosion, another bomb blew up in a residential area in the southeast section of the Salt Lake Valley. A Latter-day Saint wife and mother, Kathleen Webb Sheets, was killed when she picked up a booby-trapped package which had been left in her driveway. Sister Sheets's husband, Gary, was a former business partner of Steven Christensen, and initially there was speculation that some disgruntled investor was responsible for the killings.

Another life was probably saved from the same fate that befell the first two victims when a bomb that investigators believed was intended for a third victim prematurely exploded and seriously injured the man responsible for the tragedies. The murderer later claimed it was a suicide attempt, but few believe this to be true.

As the investigation unfolded, police discovered that documents dealer Mark W. Hofmann had concocted an elaborate forgery scheme that ultimately led him to commit the murders that claimed the lives of Steven Christensen and Kathleen Sheets.

Hofmann initially came into the public eye in 1980 when he allegedly made the first of a series of startling discoveries that purported to be early documents impacting both Latter-day Saint and United States history. Over the next five years he "discovered" more historical documents than most document dealers find in a lifetime of painstaking search.

Many of these so-called discoveries were aimed at discrediting The Church of Jesus Christ of Latter-day Saints. The forger-murderer would later admit that he deliberately set about to distort the early history of the restored Church.

As Hofmann brought forth his forged documents, critics of the Latter-day Saints gloated over seeming discrepancies in official Church accounts of marvelous manifestations from heaven. Some who were weak in the faith saw their sandy spiritual foundations disappear under the barrage of criticism.

Mark Hofmann's victims were not confined to the two whose lives he had physically taken. There were other potentially more serious victims of his deceit—those who suffered from the spiritual sickness and death that he spread through his treachery.

Although initially denying the charges brought against him, Hofmann finally confessed to the crimes in a plea-bargaining exchange with the prosecution. He admitted to making his first bomb at the age of twelve and of successfully counterfeiting a coin at the age of fifteen. This was about the time he claimed he lost his faith and became an atheist, although he continued to maintain the outward appearance of a God-fearing, religious individual for the next fifteen years of his life.

In this respect one is reminded of the Savior's rebuke to ancient hypocrites, "who make yourselves appear unto men that ye would not commit the least sin, and yet ye yourselves, transgress the whole law" (JST, Matthew 23:21).

As he became increasingly successful in his forgeries, he relished the fame and money it brought. He rationalized that if others accepted one of his forgeries as genuine, "then it was genuine by definition." He was caught up in his own pride and cleverness. His perverted thinking reminds one of an ancient anti-Christ named Korihor, who similarly followed the master of deceit and father of lies:

"I have taught [Lucifer's lying] words," Korihor confessed, "and I have taught them because they were pleasing unto the carnal mind; and I taught them, even until I had much success, insomuch that I verily believed that they were true; and for this cause

I withstood the truth, even until I have brought this great curse upon me" (Alma 30:53).

According to a newspaper account based on a transcript of Hofmann's testimony, "greed and fame drove him to the brink of financial ruin and into a bind where murder and suicide seemed the only way out. In a desperate bid to avoid being detected as a forger, he planted a home-made bomb outside the office of Steven F. Christensen, a historic-document collector who had discovered Hofmann's deceptions [and was about to make them known]. A second bomb, that he insists was meant as a diversion, killed Kathleen Webb Sheets." (CN, 8 Aug. 1987, p. C 13.)

Some might argue that the two murdered victims of Hofmann's satanical scheme were not martyrs in the sense that they did not necessarily die for their religion. I would take strong issue with that argument. Both were the victims of a deliberate effort by a modern anti-Christ to undermine the cause of Christ by discrediting His Church, His leaders, and His priesthood.

I recall hearing at least one speaker at the funeral of my fallen friend Steven Christensen speak of him as a martyr. I believe the Spirit bore witness on that occasion of the truthfulness of that inspired declaration.

One small but significant sequel should be added to this tragic story. After Hofmann had been found guilty, sentenced, and taken from the courtroom, "Mac Christensen, Steven Christensen's father, went up to Hofmann's father and embraced him. 'I told him our love was with him and his family,' said Mac Christensen. 'He cried. He didn't have to say he was sorry for what his son had done to my son. I knew he was. I could tell from his expression.' " (CN, 31 Jan. 1987, p. C 3.) This was a magnanimous act by one whose son exemplified that same loving and forgiving spirit throughout his brief earthly life.

Martyrdoms Continue Among Missionaries

The next martyr to die a violent death in the mission field was Elder James Daniel Heinze. While walking on the sidewalk in Luxembourg, Elder Heinze was killed on 11 February 1986 when struck by a car driven by a drunk driver. Elder Roger Todd Hunt was killed the following year in Amadora, Portugal, as the result of what was determined to be an accidental shooting. Two other missionaries were shot that same year in Michigan but survived the attack.

Two years later, two more missionaries would not be as fortunate. On 24 May 1989, while returning to their apartment in La Paz, Bolivia, two Elders were deliberately gunned down in a hail of bullets fired from automatic weapons. Elder Jeffrey Brent Ball of Coalville, Utah, and Elder Todd Ray Wilson of Wellington, Utah, were the victims of what was termed a "political assassination."

A maverick and radical terrorist group known as the Armed Liberation Front of Zarate Willka claimed responsibility for the unprovoked attack on the two innocent Elders. The missionaries were evidently chosen at random by terrorists who wanted to make a murderous public statement. A Church spokesman said, "They were the first politically motivated killings of Mormon missionaries in memory" (DN, 25 May 1989, A 1).

One tragic aspect of these senseless killings was that the missionaries and the Church they represented were not involved in politics at all. "It's a terrible unprovoked attack on innocent victims who have nothing to do with the political and social philosophies of this or any other group," said their mission president (CN, 27 May 1989, C 4).

There was some speculation that the Elders may have been victims of the hateful vengeance of drug czars in Bolivia whose illicit trade had been threatened by Bolivia's government with the support of the United States. Another possible explanation for the killings was given by a spokesman for the United States House of Representatives Foreign Affairs Committee: "Missionaries agitate both the left and right: the left, because they represent anticommunist America; the right because they proselytize the Indians, and [those on the right] want them left alone and unchanged. The right includes the big landowners and mine owners." (DN, 26 May 1989, A 1.)

As part of a statement of sympathy regarding the tragic slayings, the First Presidency of the Church said: "We regret that anyone would think that these representatives of The Church of Jesus Christ of Latter-day Saints who have been sent to preach the gospel of peace would be characterized as enemies of any group" (DN, 25 May 1989, A 1).

The irony of the whole affair is that these two missionaries, both known for their great love of the Bolivian people, had come to South America on a mission of peace with no other thought in mind than to preach a gospel of love. They were gunned down in La Paz, which translated means "The Peace."

Speaking at the funeral of Elder Wilson, President Gordon B. Hinckley said: "I believe Todd has not tasted any bitterness in his passing. Peace has come to him—a peace we know little of, that which is certain and good and beautiful." (DN, 31 May 1989, A 1.)

Not many years ago the Lord declared: "And it shall come to pass that those that die in me shall not taste of death, for it shall be sweet unto them" (D&C 42:46).

Though the bleeding physical remains of the martyred missionaries remained as brutal evidence of their deaths, their spirits were quickly transferred to another sphere of exquisite peace. Speaking at the funeral service for Elder Ball, President Thomas S. Monson said: "Jeff has gone home. He has gone home to God. He has gone home on a missionary transfer, and he will continue to spread the gospel. . . .

"This young man whom we honor today is still on his mission. He has not been released; he carries on the spirit of missionary work [beyond the veil]." (DN, 31 May 1989, A 1.)

President Monson suggested that if the young missionary could speak to his parents he might say, "Do not grieve, Mother; do not sorrow, Father. I am on the Lord's errand, and he may do with me as he sees fit." (SLT, 31 May 1989, B 3.)

While a venomous terrorist may strike down an innocent and unsuspecting victim, the effect of such a heinous act will be limited. The work of the martyr will simply be transferred to another sphere, where it will continue unabated by the evil one and his emissaries of hate and violence.

Furthermore, the untimely death of a disciple of Christ will have far-reaching positive effects. Many who might not have otherwise heard of the message the martyr was preaching will have their hearts touched and will join with the faithful in embracing the gospel of Jesus Christ. In this respect we reflect upon the slayings of some ancient disciples of Christ and the impact it had on nonbelievers: "And it came to pass that the people of God were joined that day by more than the number who had been slain" (Alma 24:26).

Thus, while we are saddened in the deaths of these two faithful Elders, we may with fervent faith in the reality of God's plan cry, "O death, where is thy sting? O grave, where is thy victory?" (1 Corinthians 15:55.)

Another ironic twist to the tragedy of La Paz occurred just two months after the slayings of Elders Ball and Wilson. On 23 July 1989, a car accident claimed the life of yet another missionary in the Bolivian mission. Elder Ronald J. Eastland, who had been interviewed extensively by the news media at the time of the slayings of his fellow missionaries, was killed when the car in which he was riding overturned on the outskirts of La Paz.

An appropriate conclusion to this chapter on twentieth-century martyrs might be this newspaper editorial regarding the two martyred missionaries in Bolivia: "May [we all] remember not just the grim facts of international political life reflected in the deaths of Jeffrey Brent Ball and Todd Ray Wilson but also the happier lessons reflected in their willingness to serve others and the other fine principles they stood for. Remember, in other words, that *what counts is not how they died but how they lived.* So it is with all of us." (DN, 26 May 1989, A 8; italics added.)

158

Conclusion: The Doors of Carthage Are Not Closed

The Coming Trials

In an address at the April 1980 general conference of The Church of Jesus Christ of Latter-day Saints, Elder Bruce R. McConkie, one of those sustained by the Church as a prophet, seer, and revelator, declared: "Nor are the days of our greatest sorrows and our deepest sufferings all behind us. They too lie ahead. We shall yet face greater perils, we shall yet be tested with more severe trials, and we shall yet weep more tears of sorrow than we have ever known before. . . . There will yet be martyrs; the doors in Carthage shall again enclose the innocent." (En, May 1980, 71, 73.)

Elder McConkie's allusion to the "doors in Carthage" had symbolic reference to the 1844 tragedy that took the lives of two of God's noblemen, Joseph and Hyrum Smith. Present and future Saints of God may not be literally locked up in jails—there to be slaughtered like innocent, caged creatures, as were the Prophet and the Patriarch—but more lives will yet be taken by those who oppose Christ and His servants.

Speaking at the funeral services of a missionary-martyr in 1884, President George Q. Cannon made the following observations:

It is not a new thing in the history of the work of the last days for the blood of innocence to be shed; but the frequency of these occurrences does not take away from the anguish and the sorrow, and those poignant feelings that are created by such atrocious acts. We cannot become reconciled to these things sufficiently, fortify ourselves as we may, to escape feeling upon occasions of this character that we are all liable at any time to be called to lay down our lives for the truth's sake. . . .

[Christ] never at any time led those who received the Gospel to anticipate that their fate would be any better than his, for every man and woman was taught that if the principles were what we believed them to be, that which he testified they were, it was worthy of their lives, and of every other sacrifice they might be called to make. Men, therefore, in espousing the Gospel of Jesus Christ in these last days, espouse it, as a general rule, with a full knowledge of the consequences involved therein. They have not been told that their pathway would be strewn with flowers, that they would be surrounded with ease and comfort, and that they would have friends on every hand and be popular; but where faithful Elders have gone out preaching the Gospel, they have gone declaring unto the inhabitants of the earth that the same sacrifice which had been called for in ancient days, when Jesus communicated His gospel unto men—that the same sacrifices might still, in all probability, be demanded of them, and they have been told not to hold their lives dear unto them, but for the sake of the great riches which God had bestowed, and the great and glorious reward that He had promised, they should be willing, if it were necessary, and God should require such sacrifice at their hands, to lay down their lives for the truth. (JD 25:276–77.)

Missionary Work and the Future

In addition to the deaths yet to be suffered by murdered martyrs, there will be those martyrs who will die of natural consequences while serving missions. As tens of thousands of additional missionaries are called into service in preparation for the Second Coming, there will be an increasing number who will die in the mission field.

Commenting on the risks involved in missionary work in the past, and in anticipation of future dangers, Elder M. Russell Ballard observed that "missionaries have not participated in this great work without serious challenges, tribulations, and difficulties. Parents of missionaries have always known the risk of losing a loved one serving in the mission field due to accident or illness. Now, we must add to the risk of missionary service the possibility of acts of terrorism. Terrorism is centuries old but perhaps has never before been so open and blatant nor had such extensive news coverage." (En, November 1989, 33.)

The Church takes every precaution to ensure the safety and health of the missionaries, and there is no question that the Lord has protected countless of His servants through the years. "However," Elder Ballard noted,

in a world of free agency, the Church cannot eliminate all risk nor guarantee absolutely that a missionary never will be ill, injured, or harmed. . . .

The battle to bring souls unto Christ began in the premortal world with the war in heaven. (See Rev. 12:7.) That same battle continues today in the conflict between right and wrong and between the gospel and false principles. The members of the Church hold a front-line position in the contest for the souls of men. The missionaries are on the battlefield fighting with the sword of truth to carry the glorious message of the restoration of the gospel of Jesus Christ to the peoples of the earth. No war has ever been free of risk. The prophecies of the last days lead me to believe that the intensity of the battle for the souls of men will increase and the risks will become greater as we draw closer to the second coming of the Lord. (En, November 1989, 34.)

One should not be overly concerned about the dangers or risks involved in missionary service. Church records indicate that the number of deaths of missionaries is significantly small in comparison to the total number who are serving.

After the murders of Elders Ball and Wilson in May 1989, Elder Ballard noted that "since the day of the Prophet Joseph Smith, we've had approximately 447,969 missionaries serve in the world.

161

Of those [some] 525 have lost their lives while serving as full-time missionaries." (DN, May 31, 1989, A 1.)

While the number of deaths of missionaries is comparatively low considering the total number who have served, even the loss of one is cause for sorrow. Yet we trust in the Lord, knowing that His love and watch care are infinite. The death of any missionary or servant of God will redound to good. The work of the Creator will not be frustrated (D&C 3:1).

Before the coming of the Lord, "this gospel of the kingdom shall be preached in all the world for a witness unto all nations" (Matthew 24:14). The startling events that shook the Communist world in Eastern Europe in 1989, breaking down barriers and paving the way for expanded missionary work, are but a prelude to what the future shall bring.

Speaking at a religious educators' symposium in 1979, Elder Bruce R. McConkie prophetically stated: "Some day, in the providence of the Lord, we shall get into Red China and Russia and the Middle East, and so on, until eventually the gospel will have been preached everywhere, to all people; and this will occur before the second coming of the Son of Man."

Elder McConkie went on to proclaim that "before the Lord comes, in all those nations we will have congregations that are stable, secure, devoted, and sound. We will have progressed in spiritual things to the point where they have received all of the blessings of the house of the Lord." (RES, 3.)

In a later general conference address Elder McConkie said: "We see the Lord break down the barriers so that the world of Islam and the world of Communism can hear the message of the restoration. . . .

"We see congregations of the covenant people worshipping the Lord in Moscow and Peking and Saigon. We see Saints of the Most High raising their voices in Egypt and India and Africa." (En, May 1980, 72.)

Two Prophet-Martyrs

One of the significant events preceding the Second Coming will be the emergence of two great latter-day witnesses of Jesus

162

Christ who will "prophesy a thousand two hundred and three-score days" (Revelation 11:3).

These two prophets "are to be raised up to the Jewish nation in the last days, at the time of the restoration, and to prophesy to the Jews after they are gathered and have built the city of Jerusalem in the land of their fathers" (D&C 77:15).

> Their ministry will take place after the latter-day temple has been built in Old Jerusalem, after some of the Jews who dwell there have been converted, and just before Armageddon and the return of the Lord Jesus. How long will they minister in Jerusalem and in the Holy Land? For three and a half years, the precise time spent by the Lord in his ministry to the ancient Jews. The Jews, as an assembled people, will hear again the testimony of legal administrators bearing record that salvation is in Christ and in his gospel. Who will these witnesses be? We do not know, except that they will be followers of Joseph Smith; they will hold the holy Melchizedek Priesthood; they will be members of The Church of Jesus Christ of Latter-day Saints. It is reasonable to suppose, knowing how the Lord has always dealt with his people in all ages, that they will be two members of the Council of the Twelve or of the First Presidency of the Church. (Mill M, 390.)

John the Revelator has told us that these two prophets will have the "power to shut heaven, that it rain not in the days of their prophecy: and have power over waters to turn them to blood, and to smite the earth with all plagues, as often as they will" (Revelation 11:6). The enemies of righteousness will be unsuccessful in their efforts to slay the two prophets during their three-and-one-half-year ministry.

When their mission is complete—"when they shall have finished their testimony"—Satan's mortal disciples will kill the prophets and leave them lying in the streets of Jerusalem for three days while the wicked of the world rejoice. Such rejoicing will be short-lived, for at the end of three and one-half days the prophets will rise from the dead and respond to the voice from heaven inviting them to ascend. A great earthquake will follow their ascension, separating the Mount of Olives. Many of the wicked will be destroyed and the way will be opened for the beleaguered Jewish people to escape their enemies. (Revelation 11:7–13; DCE, 606–7; ST, 170.) The Savior's second coming will be imminent.

The Nature of Martyrs

From Abel to the two unnamed prophets of the last days, martyrs of the kingdom have possessed and will possess certain character strengths that it would be well for all disciples of Christ to cultivate. One of these major characteristics is an ability to place full trust in the Lord and His purposes, regardless of what the earthly outcome may be.

Alma's response to the danger of death is typical of such an attitude: "Be it according to the will of the Lord" (Alma 14:13).

"The righteous live by faith," said Elder Marion D. Hanks. He then noted that "faith is not an easy solution to life's problems. Faith is confidence and trust in the character and purposes of God."

Elder Hanks cautioned that "the solutions that we wish and pray for do not always come about. The power that remade Paul, that poured in love and washed out hostility and hate, did not save him from the great travails, from Nero's dungeon or a martyr's death. Christ lived in him, he said, he had found the peace of God that passed all comprehension." (En, May 1975, 14.)

The Apostle Paul and all faithful persecuted and martyred Saints throughout history have been able to proclaim, "The Lord gave, and the Lord hath taken away; blessed be the name of the Lord" (see Job 1:21).

To exercise such faith, one practices the law of sacrifice. According to Elder Bruce R. McConkie, "The law of sacrifice is that we are willing to sacrifice all that we have for the truth's sake— our character and reputation; our honor and applause; our good name among men; our house, lands, and families: all things, even our very lives if need be."

Elder McConkie then added this observation: "Few of us are called upon to sacrifice much of what we possess, and at the moment there is only an occasional martyr in the cause of revealed religion. But . . . to gain celestial salvation we must be *able* to live these laws to the full if we are called upon to do so." (En, May 1975, 50.)

True disciples of Christ are not only willing to die for Him, they are also willing to live for Him. They do not put limitations on their service in the kingdom and their love of God and of their fellowmen. They love and serve with *all* their "heart, might, mind and strength" (D&C 4:2).

Elder Robert D. Hales noted that "it is not in death or in one event that we give our lives, but in every day as we are asked to do it" (En, May 1975, 44).

Can You See Them?

Saints of God and disciples of Christ will be ever grateful for the many martyrs, as well as others, who have sacrificed so much over the years to ensure that we today enjoy the blessings of the gospel of Jesus Christ. Foremost, of course, among the martyrs is the Savior Himself. Without His atoning sacrifice we would be without hope.

We can show our love and appreciation to these marvelous martyrs through the way we live our lives today and the way in which we safeguard and share the gospel with others.

In contemplating the present and the future, consider the following insights provided by Elder Loren C. Dunn:

> The story is told that toward the end of World War II an allied general came to the front lines one night to inspect his troops. As he walked along he would point out into no-man's-land and say, "Can you see them? Can you see them?"
>
> Finally, someone said, "General, we can see nothing. What do you mean?" He said, "Can't you see them? They're your buddies; they are the ones who gave their lives today, yesterday, and the day before. They're out there alright, watching you, wondering what you are going to do; wondering if they have died in vain."
>
> My dear brothers and sisters, as members of this Church we can ask ourselves the same question, "Can you see them?" They are the ones who paid, and some with their

165

lives, that the gospel of the kingdom might be established in these, the last days. . . . I am sure they are allowed to look in on us from time to time to see how the work is going, to see what we are doing with their spiritual heritage, to see if they have died in vain. (En, May 1975, 27.)

The Lord's Promises

Perhaps a fitting conclusion to this overview of the martyrs of the kingdom would be the words of the Lord Jesus Christ and of two of His apostolic witnesses:

And all they who have given their lives for my name shall be crowned (D&C 101:15).

It is a faithful saying: For if we be dead with him, we shall also live with him:

If we suffer [endure, remain constant], we shall also reign with him: if we deny him, he also will deny us. (2 Timothy 2:11–12.)

Let us seek as a people to be prepared to meet death, to flinch not from the path of duty, from the path of honor, from the path that God has marked out for us to walk in; let us tread it unfalteringly, and trust to God to preserve and deliver us, or if it be His wisdom to permit our blood to be mingled with the blood of other martyrs in testimony of the truth, may we be prepared therefor (George Q. Cannon, JD 25:280).

Bibliography

And Should We Die. Salt Lake City: The Church of Jesus Christ of Latter-day Saints, n.d.

Allen, James B., and Glen M. Leonard. *The Story of the Latter-day Saints.* Salt Lake City: Deseret Book Co., 1976.

Anderson, Nels. *Desert Saints.* Chicago: University of Chicago Press, 1966.

Arrington, Leonard J. and Davis Bitton. *The Mormon Experience.* New York: Alfred Knopf, 1979.

Backman, Milton V., Jr. *The Heavens Resound.* Salt Lake City: Deseret Book Co., 1983.

Berrett, William E. *The Restored Church.* Salt Lake City: Deseret Book Co., 1963.

Berrett, William E., and Alma P. Burton. *Readings in LDS Church History from Original Manuscripts.* 3 vols. Salt Lake City: Deseret Book Co., 1955–58.

Bible Dictionary. Salt Lake City: The Church of Jesus Christ of Latter-day Saints, 1979.

Brewster, Hoyt W., Jr. *Doctrine and Covenants Encyclopedia.* Salt Lake City: Bookcraft, 1988.

Brigham Young University Studies. Provo, Utah: Brigham Young University Press.

BIBLIOGRAPHY

Church News. Salt Lake City: The Church of Jesus Christ of Latter-day Saints.

Clark, James R., ed. *Messages of the First Presidency.* 6 vols. Salt Lake City: Bookcraft, 1965–75.

Conference Reports. Salt Lake City: The Church of Jesus Christ of Latter-day Saints.

Cowan, Richard O. *The Church in the Twentieth Century.* Salt Lake City: Bookcraft, 1985.

Deseret News. Salt Lake City.

Devotional Speeches of the Year. Provo, Utah: Brigham Young University.

Ensign. Salt Lake City: The Church of Jesus Christ of Latter-day Saints.

Fox's Book of Martyrs. W. B. Forbush, ed. New York: Holt, Rinehart and Winston, 1954.

Godfrey, Kenneth, et al. *Women's Voices.* Salt Lake City: Deseret Book Co., 1982.

Grant, Carter E. *The Kingdom of God Restored.* Salt Lake City: Deseret Book Co., 1955.

Hatch, Nelle Spilsbury. *Colonia Juárez.* Salt Lake City: Deseret Book Co., 1954.

Hatch, William W. *There Is No Law.* New York: Vantage Press, 1968.

Hinckley, Bryant S. *Life of a Great Leader.* Salt Lake City: Deseret Book Co., 1951.

Improvement Era. Salt Lake City: The Church of Jesus Christ of Latter-day Saints.

Jenson, Andrew. *LDS Biographical Encyclopedia.* 4 vols. Salt Lake City: Western Epics, 1971.

Journal of Discourses. 26 vols. London: Latter-day Saints' Book Depot, 1854–86.

Juvenile Instructor. Salt Lake City: The Church of Jesus Christ of Latter-day Saints.

Larson, Gustive O. *The "Americanization" of Utah for Statehood.* San Marino, California: Huntington Library, 1971.

Latter-day Sentinel. Arizona edition.

Lycurgus, A. Wilson. *Life of David W. Patten: The First Apostolic Martyr.* Salt Lake City: Deseret News, 1900.

McConkie, Bruce R. *Doctrinal New Testament Commentary.* 3 vols. Salt Lake City: Bookcraft, 1965–73.

———. *The Millennial Messiah.* Salt Lake City: Deseret Book Co., 1982.

———. *Mormon Doctrine.* 2d ed. Salt Lake City: Bookcraft, 1966.

———. *The Mortal Messiah.* 4 vols. Salt Lake City: Deseret Book Co., 1979–81.

McGavin, E. Cecil. *Nauvoo the Beautiful.* Salt Lake City: Stevens and Wallis, 1946.

McKay, David O. *Ancient Apostles.* Salt Lake City: Deseret Book Co., 1964.

Millennial Star. Manchester, England: The Church of Jesus Christ of Latter-day Saints.

Oaks, Dallin H., and Marvin S. Hill. *Carthage Conspiracy.* Urbana, Illinois: University of Illinois Press, 1975.

Patton, Annaleone D. *California Mormons.* Salt Lake City: Deseret Book Co., 1961.

Peloubet, F. N. *Peloubet's Bible Dictionary.* Philadelphia: Universal Book and Bible House, 1947.

Pratt, Parley P. *Autobiography of Parley P. Pratt.* Salt Lake City: Deseret Book Co., 1966.

Religious Educators' Symposium. Salt Lake City: Church Education System, The Church of Jesus Christ of Latter-day Saints, 1979.

Reynolds, George, and Janne M. Sjodahl. *Commentary on the Pearl of Great Price.* Salt Lake City: Deseret Book Co., 1980.

Rich, Russell R. *Ensign to the Nations.* Provo, Utah: Brigham Young University Press, 1972.

Roberts, B. H. *A Comprehensive History of The Church of Jesus Christ of Latter-day Saints.* 6 vols. Provo, Utah: The Church of Jesus Christ of Latter-day Saints, 1930.

———. *The Life of John Taylor.* Salt Lake City: Bookcraft, 1963.

———. *The Missouri Persecutions.* Salt Lake City: Bookcraft, 1965.

———. *The Rise and Fall of Nauvoo.* Salt Lake City: Bookcraft, 1965.

Romney, Thomas C. *The Mormon Colonies in Mexico.* Salt Lake City: Deseret Book Co., 1938.

Salt Lake Tribune. Salt Lake City.

Scharffs, Gilbert W. *Mormonism in Germany.* Salt Lake City: Deseret Book Co., 1970.

Smith, Joseph. *History of the Church of Jesus Christ of Latter-day Saints.* 2d ed., rev. Edited by B. H. Roberts. 7 vols. Salt Lake City: The Church of Jesus Christ of Latter-day Saints, 1932–51.

————. *Teachings of the Prophet Joseph Smith.* Compiled by Joseph Fielding Smith. Salt Lake City: Deseret Book Co., 1938.

Smith, Joseph Fielding. *Doctrines of Salvation.* Compiled by Bruce R. McConkie. 3 vols. Salt Lake City: Bookcraft, 1954–56.

————. *Essentials in Church History.* Salt Lake City: Deseret Book Co., 1979.

————. *The Signs of the Times.* Salt Lake City: Deseret Book Co., 1961.

————. *The Way to Perfection.* Salt Lake City: Deseret Book Co., 1931.

Smith, Lucy Mack. *History of Joseph Smith.* Edited by Preston Nibley. Salt Lake City: Bookcraft, 1958.

Southern Star. Chatanooga, Tennessee: Southern States Mission of The Church of Jesus Christ of Latter-day Saints, 1898–1900.

Speeches of the Year. Provo, Utah: Brigham Young University, 1973.

Talmage, James E. *Jesus the Christ.* 25th ed. Salt Lake City: Deseret Book Co., 1956.

Times and Seasons. Nauvoo, Illinois: The Church of Jesus Christ of Latter-day Saints.

Tullidge, Edward W. *The Women of Mormondom.* New York, 1877.

Whitney, Orson F. *Popular History of Utah.* Salt Lake City: Deseret News Press, 1916.

Young, Brigham. *Manuscript History of Brigham Young, 1801–1844.* Compiled by Elden J. Watson. Salt Lake City, 1967.

Young, John R. *Memoirs of John R. Young, Utah Pioneer, 1847.* Salt Lake City: Deseret News Press, 1920.

Young Woman's Journal. Salt Lake City: The Church of Jesus Christ of Latter-day Saints.

Index

171

INDEX

Darley, Gary, 150
David, 13
Dempsey, John, 142
Denmark, 139, 147
Detroit, Michigan, 143
DeWitt, Missouri, 92
Díaz, Porfirio, 143-44
Dibble, Philo, 88
Dixon, Illinois, 70-71
Doctrine and Covenants, 84
Domitian, 26
Doniphan, Alexander W., 68
Dunn, Loren C., 139; on martyrs, 165-66
Durfee, Edmund, 99

Earthquakes, 143, 163
Eastern States Mission, 120, 145
Eastland, Ronald J., 158
Ebed-melech, 15
Eden, 9, 34
Edmunds, George F., 123
Edmunds bill, 123
Edmunds-Tucker bill, 124-25
Edwards, Edward, 114
Egypt, 18, 61, 162
El Cajon, California, 152
Elias, 45
Eliason, Henry, 152
Elijah, 14
Elisha, 17
Elk Mountains, 113
Emigrants, 3, 106
Endurance, 6
England, 139, 142, 149
Enoch, 38
Ensign, Elias, 107
Ensign, Eliza, 107
Eternal life, 2-3
Ether, 56
Eugene, West Virginia, 142
Europe, 146-47; Eastern, 162
Eve, 9-10
Evil spirits, 70
Ewing, Finis, 86
Excommunications, 149
Extermination order, 94

Fairview, Utah, 139
Faith, 1, 2, 6, 34, 53, 55, 62, 89, 93, 96, 106-7, 112, 117, 119, 120, 139, 140, 154, 164
Fall of Adam, 34
Far West, Missouri, 92, 93
Fayette, New York, 83
Featherstone, Vaughn J., on martyred missionaries, 152

First Presidency, 84, 138, 146, 149, 163; on martyred missionaries, 156-57; on World War II, 148
First Vision, 62
Fischer, Mark, 150
Flood, 11
Florence, Nebraska, 102, 108
Florida, 136
Ford, Thomas, 74-76
Foreordination, 63
Forgeries, 152-55
Forgiveness, 22, 43
Fort Hall Indian Reservation, 151
Fowler, Jerusha, child of, 107
France, 1, 145
Fuller, Josiah, 95

Gabriel, 19
Gallatin, Missouri, 92
Garden Grove, Iowa, 101
Gathering, 163
Georgia, 129-30, 137
Germany, 139, 142, 145-49
Gestapo, 146-47, 149
Gethsemane, 22, 28, 33-35, 41, 45
Gibbs, John H., 132-35
Gideon, 50
Gilbert, Whitney, and Company (store), 88
God, 17; justice of, 148, 151; trust in, 162, 164, 166. See also Heavenly Father; Jesus Christ
Golden plates, 65-66
Golgotha, 42
Goodwin, Laura, 107
Grand River, 92
Grant, Caroline, 113
Grant, George W., 110
Grant, Jedediah M., 113
Grant, Ulysses S., 122
Greenwood, Robert, 150
Grow, David, 150

Hale, Nathan, 1
Hales, Robert D., on sacrifice, 165
Hamburg, Germany, 149
Hamlin, Mary, 129
Hammer, Austin, 95
Hancock County, Illinois, 99
Handcart pioneers, 107-10
Hanks, Marion D., on faith, 164
Hansen, William M., 136-37
Harrent County, North Carolina, 136
Harrisburg, Illinois, 151
Hatred, 40, 43
Haun's Mill Massacre, 94-96

173